TURNING POINTS

I0884137

By Simon Pierce

THE GREAT DEPRESSION

Cavendish Square

New York

Published in 2021 by Cavendish Square Publishing, LLC
243 5th Avenue, Suite 136, New York, NY 10016

First Edition

Portions of this work were originally authored by Don Nardo and published as *The Great Depression* (*American History*). All new material this edition authored by Simon Pierce.

All websites were available and accurate when this book was sent to press.

Cataloging-in-Publication Data

Names: Pierce, Simon.
Title: The Great Depression / Simon Pierce.
Description: New York : Cavendish Square, 2021. | Series: Turning points | Includes index.
Identifiers: ISBN 9781502657657 (pbk.) | ISBN 9781502657664 (library bound) | ISBN 9781502657671 (ebook)
Subjects: LCSH: Depressions–1929–United States–Juvenile literature. | New Deal, 1933-1939–Juvenile literature. | United States–History–1933-1945–Juvenile literature. | United States–History–1919-1933–Juvenile literature. | United States–Economic conditions–1918-1945–Juvenile literature.
Classification: LCC E806.P54 2021 | DDC 330.9730916–dc23

Editor: Jennifer Lombardo
Copy Editor: Michelle Denton
Designer: Deanna Paternostro

Some of the images in this book illustrate individuals who are models. The depictions do not imply actual situations or events.

CPSIA compliance information: Batch #CS20CSQ: For further information contact Cavendish Square Publishing LLC, New York, New York at 1-877-980-4450.

Printed in the United States of America

TABLE OF CONTENTS

SPORTS ★ FINAL
DAILY NEWS
50¢
2.5 MILLION READERS EVERY DAY
NYDailyNews.com
SHOCK MARKET
CRISIS ON WALL STREET
Dow plunges 504 points
Insurance giant teeters on brink
Fear as traders await opening bell
FULL COVERAGE ON PAGES 2-6 & BUSINESS
116

INTRODUCTION

A WORLDWIDE STRUGGLE

Most countries around the world have a partially or entirely capitalist economy. In this system, goods and services are sold by individuals or private companies rather than controlled by the government. To keep a capitalist economy working, people must buy things. This gives businesses money to pay their workers, who can then go out and buy things from other companies, and the cycle continues. If people stop buying things or reduce the amount they buy, the system slows down and eventually collapses.

All capitalist economies have experienced this boom-bust cycle numerous times. One of the most recent American bust periods, which has been termed the Great Recession, occurred between 2007 and 2009. During this financial crisis, hundreds of thousands of people lost their jobs, millions of people lost money, and nearly everyone was unhappy with the state of the economy. Although economists declared the recession over in 2009, its effects were felt for years. Many people have predicted that another recession will occur in the future, in part because of the loss of confidence in businesses that occurred during the last recession.

Although recessions are difficult for people to endure, they are less severe than economic depressions. Part of the reason why the

In September 2008, a huge stock market dip occurred. This was one of the most visible signs of the economic recession, although it had been brewing for more than a year.

2007 economic collapse was a recession rather than a depression was that, as government officials saw signs that it was coming, they did their best to prepare for it. Because of this, the effects of a total collapse were avoided, and though the financial impact was still large, it could have been much worse. The country was able to recover relatively quickly. The Great Depression, on the other hand, was a crippling disaster not only because of the initial economic failure but also because it took about a decade—from 1929 to 1939—for the government to repair the market.

A Global Disaster

The Great Depression affected multiple countries, not just the United States. Because the world's economies have become increasingly interconnected over the years, such a disaster often has ripple effects. When a country has to spend money to take care of its own citizens, it has less money for international trade, causing economic troubles in countries that suddenly have difficulty finding an overseas market for their goods and services. In fact, part of the reason why the Great Depression lasted as long as it did was because many countries raised tariffs, or taxes, on imported goods in an effort to encourage their citizens to buy things that were made in their own country. The intention was to improve the economy of the country by keeping money flowing into domestic businesses rather than ones overseas, but since most countries adopted such policies, they all suffered from decreased international trade.

In fact, one of the most devastating consequences of the Great Depression was the rise of the Nazi Party and the Holocaust in Germany. Jews were targeted by the government and largely blamed for the country's misfortunes. Many German citizens were scared and struggling, so they were happy to have someone to blame and elected a leader—Adolf Hitler—who promised to do something about it. When German Jews started to experience discrimination, some tried to leave the country. However, the United States and other countries had tightened immigration rules in response to the Great Depression. Additionally, one of the policies the Nazis enacted

Germany was already dealing with economic problems when the Great Depression hit. These economic troubles helped Adolf Hitler (*shown here*) gain power with promises to improve the German economy.

before establishing concentration camps was that Jews who wanted to leave the country had to leave behind all their money and possessions, which were seen as the property of Germany. The United States Holocaust Memorial Museum explained:

> *In the 1930s, when the Nazis began stripping Jews of their financial holdings prior to allowing them to immigrate, many had trouble passing the rigorous [strict] financial qualifications for entry to America. Throughout the 1930s, the majority of Americans opposed increasing immigration to the United States. Many cited economic concerns, fearing that immigrants would compete for jobs, which were scarce during the Depression.*[1]

With this combination of domestic and foreign policies in place, many Jews had nowhere to go and ended up stuck in the country when the Nazis started sending them to concentration camps.

The Scope of the Crisis

Though the decade-long Great Depression was a terrible economic disaster, the United States was eventually able to do more than just recover from it. The nation emerged after World War II, which it fought in from 1941 to 1945, as the richest country in the world, and it has remained at or near the top of global wealth rankings ever since. For generations, many Americans have known nothing but economic opportunity, prosperity, and a high standard of living. For the most part, even the nation's poorest citizens don't have to live through conditions nearly as desperate as those faced by more than 10 million Americans in the midst of the Great Depression.

It is often difficult for people today to truly understand the scope and horror of the Great Depression. Merely listing the numbers of people who lost their life savings, jobs, and homes is not enough. Statistics cannot adequately convey the levels of hardship that people across the country had to endure.

Take, for example, the housing conditions during the crisis. Millions of Americans, both in cities and rural areas, lost their houses and could only afford to live in small, flimsy shacks. These shacks generally had no electricity, no running water, and no toilets. At the height of the Depression, Mary Owsley of Oklahoma reported:

[People were living] in everything from … houses built out of cardboard boxes and old pieces of metal … I knew one family there in Oklahoma City, a man and a woman and seven children lived in a hole in the ground … They had chairs and tables and beds back in that hole. And they had the dirt all braced up there, just like a cave.[2]

Many people who still had homes lived in constant fear of losing them due to their inability to pay rent. In 1932 alone, more than 270,000 American families were evicted, or forcibly removed, from their homes.

No Money for Necessities

The horrible housing situation was only one of the many components of the crisis. Because of the widespread lack of both jobs and money, many parents could not afford to buy decent clothes for either themselves or their children. Food was also difficult to come by all across the country. Various charities and religious institutions responded by setting up soup kitchens, where long lines of starving people formed every evening.

In 1932, a secretary for the Community Council of Philadelphia, Pennsylvania, testified before a Senate subcommittee about the horrible food situations he had witnessed:

One woman said she borrowed 50 cents from a friend and bought stale bread for 3 1/2 cents per loaf, and that is all [her family] had for eleven days except for one or two meals …

One woman went along the docks and picked up vegetables that fell from the wagons. Sometimes the fish vendors gave her fish at the end of the day. On two different occasions, the family was without food for a day and a half.[3]

This was not unique to Philadelphia; situations such as these were common all over the United States. Under such poor conditions, and with no end or remedy in sight, it's not surprising that many people eventually started to believe that the Depression would never end. Some people went so far as to take their own lives, and suicide rates increased during the years of the Great Depression.

It is difficult for most modern Americans to imagine these levels of hardship and desperation. How did things get so bad in the United States? Could a similar massive economic catastrophe strike the country in the future? To answer these questions, it's important to examine how the Great Depression came to be, how the government responded to it, and how the ordinary American citizen adapted

The lines for a cheap or free meal were known as "bread lines." Incredibly long bread lines, such as the one shown here, were a common sight during the Great Depression.

and survived. It is also crucial to realize that, though the Depression itself ended, its legacy will live on. In the words of historian Robert S. McElvaine, "Events in those years have determined the direction of our social and economic policies, our relationship to our government, and our political alignments ever since."[4]

CHAPTER ONE

CRASH AND BURN

It's generally agreed that the beginning of the Great Depression was the stock market crash of October 1929. However, there were many factors that led up to this event. For years, banks and stockbrokers had been investing in foolish, risky ways. The "Great Crash" was the result—in the end, their risks led to ruin.

One of the reasons why the Depression struck quickly and unexpectedly is that these banking risks paid off for a short time, so many people thought the economy was doing extremely well. Though many Americans were still poor, many more were able to enter the middle class. This was seen as undeniably positive by a large number of people. Historian Howard Zinn described this time:

> *Unemployment was down, from 4,270,000 [people] in 1921 to a little over 2 million in 1927. The general level of wages for workers rose. Some farmers made a lot of money. The 40 percent of all families who made over $2,000 a year could buy new gadgets: autos [cars], radios, refrigerators. Millions of people were not doing badly—and they could shut out of the picture the others—the tenant farmers … [and] the immigrant families in the big cities either without work or not making enough to get the basic necessities.*[1]

Many people could afford luxuries such as cars in the 1920s. This fooled them into believing these good economic times would last forever.

In addition, the wealthiest class of society saw its fortunes grow even faster than the middle class. This would eventually come to harm the general state of the economy. However, because many people were now richer, they believed the economy was in great shape. High-profile stockbrokers, who insisted that the stock market was going to be incredibly profitable, seemingly confirmed this. As a result, stock prices were at an all-time high in 1929, despite the government's attempt to keep prices down. However, this huge rise in stock prices is what eventually led to the crash on October 24, which is now remembered as Black Thursday. Though it's not possible to identify one single cause of the Great Depression, the wealth gap between the classes and the speculative investment practices of banks were undoubtedly major contributors.

The Rich Get Richer

Before the start of the Great Depression, the wealth gap, or the gap between the richest portion of Americans and the poorest, started widening—and never stopped. A 1934 study conducted by the Brookings Institution, a social policy group, found a huge rift between rich and poor in pre-Depression America. In 1929, shortly before the stock market crash, the top 0.1 percent of American families held wealth and income equal to the entire bottom 42 percent of American families. Nearly 80 percent of American families had no savings at all, while only 24,000 families held 34 percent of all the savings in the country. In other words, a huge amount of wealth was being concentrated in the hands of a relatively tiny number of people and families.

Many of the wealthiest families were the owners of massive businesses, such as the descendants of oil tycoon John D. Rockefeller or steel magnate Andrew Carnegie, and they employed millions of middle- and lower-class Americans. Big businesses were making the American economy boom, raising millions of people to the middle class and improving the general quality of life nationwide. However, this kind of economic system has one flaw that, at the time, few economists, politicians, or advisers were able to identify: What would happen if some of these families or businesses lost their fortune?

A federal income tax—a tax on the amount of money a person makes in a year—wasn't instituted in the United States until 1913, which is part of why the wealth gap had grown so big. Shown here is the mansion John D. Rockefeller built with his enormous fortune.

Because most of these companies were large and employed tens of thousands of Americans, all of those people would lose their jobs if the company went under. When one person loses their job, they are no longer creating anything to add to the nation's financial growth, and their ability to spend money is greatly diminished. If thousands of people lose their jobs all at once, there is a noticeable decrease in economic development. Moreover, if a large company fails, the stock market is impacted as well, causing millions of stockholders to lose money even if they haven't lost their own jobs.

One thing that endangered these companies was that some wealthy investors were engaging in risky business practices. For example, stock pools were common in the late 1920s. American historian Samuel E. Morison described a stock pool:

> *A group of men would get together, buy a sizable block of stock of [anything], then trade shares back and forth, hiking the price and pulling in outsiders who hoped to get in on the profits. When the*

PAST MEETS PRESENT: THE ECONOMIC CLIMATE

Many people have expressed concern about the ways the current economic climate resembles the economic climate of 1929. One of the most noticeable similarities is the large wealth gap. One-quarter of all American workers live below the national poverty line, which means they have trouble affording basic necessities. Because they have less money available, many people buy things on credit, running up high levels of credit card debt. According to CNBC, 55 percent of all Americans with credit cards have debt they can't afford to pay off. In contrast, after the country recovered from the Great Recession, people who were already rich got much richer. According to financial expert Kimberly Amadeo, "In 2012, the top 10 [percent] of earners took home 50 [percent] of all income. That's the highest percentage in the last 100 years."[1]

Despite all of these similarities, economic experts stated that as of the end of 2019, the US economy was relatively healthy. However, many expect it to start slowing down in the near future, due partially to tariffs set in place by President Donald Trump. According to Amadeo, experts are seeing signs that investors believe "another recession is probably two to three years out."[2] She cautioned investors not to immediately sell their stocks if their prices dip temporarily. Thanks to many policies set in place and lessons learned during the 1930s, an economic downturn as severe as the Great Depression is less likely to materialize in the next several years.

1. Kimberly Amadeo, "Income Inequality in America," The Balance, modified December 16, 2019, www.thebalance.com/income-inequality-in-america-3306190.

2. Amadeo, "US Economic Outlook for 2019 and Beyond," The Balance, modified December 14, 2019, www.thebalance.com/us-economic-outlook-3305669.

stock reached an agreed point, members of the pool dumped it on the market, took their profits, and retired, leaving the suckers to take the [loss].[2]

The federal government was actively attempting to stop this kind of market manipulation in the 1920s. Powerful stockbrokers worked around the new laws by making increasingly risky financial ventures. One common investment before the Depression was in a holding company. Holding companies don't make a product or provide a service. Rather, the operators of a holding company buy several other businesses and manage them, taking a percentage of the profit of each business. With few exceptions, it was wealthy people who were acquiring and running holding companies, selling hundreds of thousands of shares to poorer, working-class people. This would ordinarily not be a problem, but at the time, many managers used immoral or illegal strategies to run the holding companies; they often mismanaged the companies while taking money from them to fill their own pockets.

Because of this poor management, such companies had a high risk of failure, and when they went out of business, they left the investors with a collection of worthless stocks, essentially having wasted their investment. However, since holding companies were very profitable for the wealthy people who owned them, more started popping up, and many regular investors were unaware of the risk of investing in them. As these weak companies increased in number, the risk of financial ruin to thousands of investors—and to the national economy—increased along with them.

Other Problems

Financial mistakes and shady business practices were not the only contributors to the market crash and the Depression. Several other factors included the increased production of goods as well as fluctuations in consumer spending and borrowing and their effects on banks. For example, because they thought the economy would continue to expand, wealthy farmers massively overproduced their goods in the 1920s. By doing this, they created a large surplus of crops and other farm products. This had the unintended effect of dramatically lowering the prices of these products; because there were so many of them available, people weren't willing to pay as much for them. As a result, small farmers found it more difficult to make a profit because they couldn't match the production of large corporate farms, yet their prices decreased anyway thanks to the larger farms' surplus. This increased their risk of bankruptcy if the economy suddenly slowed down.

Similarly, many manufacturing industries were producing more goods than the average American could afford to buy. Because of this nationwide surplus, these companies began cutting back their production in 1928 and 1929—not long before the market crashed. Because they were producing less, they needed fewer workers, so people lost their jobs. In turn, those people who were now unemployed had to reduce their spending, which increased the surplus of the goods that they would normally have bought when they were employed. This caused companies to cut production even further, resulting in more job losses—and the vicious cycle continued.

Large farms produced so much food in the 1920s that they drove the prices for those foods down all over the country. Because of this, small farms that produced the same kind of food had difficulty competing and making a profit.

This economic climate negatively affected banks as well, partly because these now-unemployed people had to take money out of their savings accounts, which decreased the amount of money banks had available to invest. Even worse for banks, though, was the degenerating situation with credit and debt. Many struggling small farmers took out business loans, and millions of ordinary consumers bought goods on credit because they needed or wanted the goods immediately but had no money yet to buy them. Buying something on credit means that the purchaser (the borrower or debtor) takes out a small loan in order to afford the item, and slowly pays their lender (also called a creditor; this was typically their bank) back over time. This is how a credit card works: Someone pays for something by swiping their credit card, and that purchase is added to their bill. Every month, they pay for all the things they bought on credit at one time by paying their credit card bill.

Between 1925 and 1929, the amount owed to banks by borrowers more than doubled, from $1.4 billion to $3 billion. As unemployment increased, large numbers of people found themselves unable to pay back their debts. Without that income, many banks were on the verge of collapse, and some were already shut down before the 1929 market crash.

Though it appeared that the decade of the 1920s was a signal of good economic things to come, the economy was actually unstable beneath its rich exterior. In modern terms, the country was in an economic bubble. Eventually, the combined disasters of a stock market collapse, high unemployment, and a widening wealth gap caused the bubble to burst.

The Great Crash

Black Thursday happened after the New York Stock Exchange (NYSE) suffered a series of devastating blows over the course of several weeks. In October 1929, the market suddenly slumped when thousands of investors, worried that their stocks were declining in worth, sold them in large quantities. As more people dumped their stocks, a general panic set in, which led to the biggest mass sale of stock the country had ever seen.

FROM THE SOURCE: A NATION IN TORMENT

Journalist Edward R. Ellis, who lived through the Depression, summed up the economic climate before the crash in his book, *A Nation in Torment: The Great American Depression, 1929–1939*:

> *Greedy people wanted more than they needed. Foolish people thought they could get something for nothing. Impulsive people bought now in the hope of paying later. Income and wealth were distributed unfairly and dangerously ... The masses were not paid enough money to consume all the goods they produced. The economy was unsound. The corporate structure was sick. The banking system was weak. Foreign trade was out of balance ... [These] conditions left the economy a flawed and loaded gun, and when the stock market crashed, the gun did not merely fire—it exploded in everyone's face.*[1]

1. Edward R. Ellis, *A Nation in Torment: The Great American Depression, 1929–1939* (New York, NY: Coward-McCann, 1970), p. 103.

The market panic continued in the days that followed. The total amount of money lost during the decline of the pre-Depression stock market is the equivalent of hundreds of billions of dollars in the 21st century. Immediately, Americans who owned a large amount of stock were hit with financial disaster. Some of them suffered such terrible losses that they took their own lives. Arthur A. Robinson, a wealthy businessman, later recalled what happened to a successful cigar company. Robinson said, "I got a call from the company president. Could I loan him $200 million? I refused, because at the time I had to protect my own [business]. His $115 stock dropped to $2 and he jumped out of the window of his Wall Street office."[3]

Although the rich were the first ones affected by the stock market crash, they were far from the only ones who experienced financial despair. The effects of the enormous losses in the stock market rapidly spiraled outward, engulfing most of the rest of society, as historian Gerald W. Johnson explained:

> *When the panic of 1929 suddenly wiped out the whole value of many stocks and sharply reduced the values of others, a great number of people who had thought themselves rich, or at least well-off, found themselves with much less than they had thought they had, or with nothing at all. By [the] millions they quit buying anything except what they had to save to stay alive. This drop in spending threw the stores into trouble, and they quit ordering [new products] and discharged [laid off] clerks. When orders stopped, the factories shut down, and factory workers had no jobs.*[4]

This financial chain reaction was destructive to the national economy. As consumer buying significantly slowed down, many people were worried about keeping their money in banks. Thousands of people withdrew their savings and hid them under their mattresses or in their attics. People also defaulted, or failed to make payments, on their bank loans. Both of these trends fatally wounded hundreds of banks, causing them to close down due to lack of funds. When this occurred, the clients who had not yet withdrawn their savings lost them. The banks were no longer able to return their money, and no laws were in place at that time to deal with this. As banks failed, millions of people—even those who had neither invested in the stock market nor lost their jobs—were thrown into poverty.

As the disastrous collapse hit, companies both big and small laid off large portions of their workforces. Unemployment rates, which had remained fairly low at under 5 percent, rose to 9 percent by early 1930. In the next two years, the rise continued and reached a devastating 25 percent. Unemployment insurance and Social Security, which today help temporarily jobless people survive, didn't exist at the time. The government had no safety measures in place to protect citizens from this momentous collapse.

Ben Isaacs's clothing business was among those that suffered because many of his customers, most of whom owed him money, couldn't afford to pay him. Eventually, Isaacs had to go on

HISTORY HAPPENED HERE: WALL STREET

Wall Street is both a place and an idea. The place is an actual street called Wall Street in Manhattan, an island that is part of New York City. The idea is the general concept of capitalism, stock trading, and banking in relation to the US economy. Many important businesses that are central to these industries are located on Wall Street; for example, the New York Stock Exchange is located at 11 Wall Street. Other businesses are located on other streets nearby but are still considered part of the idea Wall Street represents. When people say things such as "Wall Street is worried about the economy," they mean the people who control trading and banking are worried, whether or not these people actually work on Wall Street.

Wall Street is located at the tip of the island of Manhattan in New York City.

relief—that is, accept handouts of money, food, and clothing from charities. However, because of the terrible conditions everywhere, even that did little to stop his family's downward slide:

> *I went to the relief and they … gave me $45 a month … So how long can that $45 go? I was paying $30 on the rent. I [had to] find … a cheaper [apartment], stove heat, for $15 a month … Today a dog wouldn't live in that type of a place. Such a dirty, filthy, dark place … About two months later, all of a sudden—no water. The city closed for the [landlord's] non-payment of the water bill.*
>
> *My wife used to carry two pails of water from the next-door neighbors and bring it up for us to wash the kids and to flush the toilet with it, and then wash our hands and face with it … We lived without water for almost two months.*[5]

Isaac's family was only one of millions with similar stories. People all across America desperately wondered when the crisis would end, when life would get back to normal, and when people would regain their jobs, lives, and dignity.

How You See History

1. Do you think the Great Depression could have been avoided? If so, how?
2. Do you think the United States could experience another depression? Explain your answer.
3. Why do you think the stock market crash of 1929 was such a surprise to so many Americans?

CHAPTER TWO

PRESIDENTIAL FAILURES AND SUCCESSES

In May 1930, roughly seven months after the stock market crash and the beginning of the Depression, President Herbert Hoover tried to raise people's spirits. "We have now passed the worst,"[1] he declared with confidence. At the time, the American people believed him; what reason did they have to doubt him? Most people assumed—and hoped—the crisis would pass quickly. No one predicted at first how long the Great Depression would last.

Part of the reason it lasted so long was that Hoover's administration refused to acknowledge the depth and severity of the crisis. While he couldn't avoid the fact that thousands of people were joining the ranks of the unemployed every day, Hoover believed the situation would simply resolve itself, given enough time. His top aides advised him that the market could heal on its own and that the United States would soon recover. Just as stockbrokers were promising people that things were looking up, politicians were quick to declare that recovery had started despite the fact that levels of unemployment and poverty remained high.

A Misguided Policy

Because Hoover's top officials were hesitant to identify the Depression as a full-scale crisis, his administration was slow and ineffective

Herbert Hoover became one of the most unpopular presidents in history during the Great Depression.

at fighting against it. He did eventually disagree with top political leaders and attempt to stimulate the economy, but the market was so thoroughly broken by that time that none of his initiatives were much help. This was also partially because his relief efforts were aimed at helping banks and stocks, based on the misguided assumption that the improvement of these industries would lead to an improvement for everyone. Throughout his presidency, Hoover's administration took the stance that giving free aid to the American people would destroy the economy rather than save it. This mistake had serious repercussions for the country and for his own reputation.

One of the reasons Hoover refused to help citizens at an individual level was that he believed it would weaken people's sense of

In 1932, 10,000 unemployed men from Pittsburgh, Pennsylvania, marched on Washington, DC, to demand that Herbert Hoover fix the economic crisis so they could find jobs.

THEY MADE HISTORY: HERBERT HOOVER

After graduating from Stanford University in 1895 with a degree in geology, Herbert Hoover became a successful mining engineer. After making his fortune, he began devoting much of his time to relief work for people in need. He was particularly active in programs that fed homeless and starving Europeans during World War I. In 1917, President Woodrow Wilson put him in charge of US food programs for the war effort. Hoover was a true humanitarian; he would provide aid to anyone who asked for it. He went so far as to supply food to millions of starving Russians in the aftermath of the Communist takeover in Soviet Russia. Americans, being generally anti-Communist, criticized Hoover's charity. He defended himself by declaring, "Twenty million people are starving. Whatever their politics, they shall be fed!"[1]

After making a name for himself as a humanitarian in the early 1920s, Hoover served as secretary of commerce under presidents Warren G. Harding and Calvin Coolidge. In this new position, Hoover worked to create voluntary partnerships between government, big businesses, and major private charities. He was praised for coordinating relief efforts after disastrous floods ravaged the Mississippi River valley in 1927. The following year, he ran for president and often promised in his campaign speeches to end poverty in the United States. This makes the fact that he presided over the start of the Great Depression, when poverty was more widespread than ever before, especially ironic.

1. Quoted in "Herbert Hoover," WhiteHouse.gov, accessed November 14, 2019, www.whitehouse.gov/1600/presidents/herberthoover.

spirit in the long term. The country was built on the ideas of the power of the individual and the strength of the free market. Hoover believed that if the government acted as a charity for its citizens, the American people would lose their work ethic and independence.

This philosophy was not at all helpful to people who were starving and homeless in 1930. Despite some conservative intervention by the federal government and the best efforts of business leaders nationwide, the stock market continued to suffer crashes, and the country's biggest industries were failing. The Great Depression was still at its beginning in the early 1930s, and the numbers of American poor and unemployed continued to grow.

It is important to note that Hoover was neither a totally incompetent politician nor a cruelly insensitive person. He did what he truly believed would be the best for the American people. The problem with his presidency lies mostly with the fact that his economic philosophy simply didn't work in the 1930s. It was founded on the ideas of individual hard work; a deregulated free market, meaning a capitalist economy in which the government didn't set restrictions or rules; and providing for the poor through private charitable organizations, such as the Salvation Army. Hoover's entire life before becoming president had been shaped by these and similar ideas.

This system worked so well, Hoover claimed, because the central government played a minimal role in business. This left private business owners and managers to hire and fire, manufacture and market goods, and invest their hard-earned money. For Hoover, this approach was only right for an independent, self-governing nation. "When the Federal Government undertakes to go into commercial business," Hoover warned, "it must at once set up the organization and administration of that business, and it immediately finds itself in a [maze], every alley of which leads to the destruction of self-government."[2] When big government tries to create and control industry and business, he believed, it robs individuals of the right to do so on their own. It also dangerously increases governmental power, potentially threatening people's liberty. Even after the initial onset of the Depression, the president refused to waver from this basic philosophy of self-reliance and fear of government intervention. In an early 1931 press statement, he said:

> *This is not an issue as to whether people shall go hungry or cold in the United States. It is solely a question of the best method by which hunger and cold shall be prevented. It is a question as to*

FROM THE SOURCE: HENRY FORD ON UNEMPLOYMENT

Though President Herbert Hoover was the most prominent American to encourage the poor and homeless to return to a self-reliant lifestyle, he was far from the only one. Henry Ford, founder of the Ford Motor Company, wrote an essay in 1932, advising people to grow their own food to survive:

> *Methods of self-help are numerous and great numbers of people have made the stimulating discovery that they need not depend on employers to find work for them—they can find work for themselves … The land! That is where our roots are … From the land comes everything that supports life … The land has not collapsed or shrunk in either extent or productivity. It is there waiting to honor all the labor we are willing to invest in it … Let every man and every family at this season of the year cultivate a plot of land and raise a sufficient supply for themselves or others. Every city and village has vacant space whose use would be permitted.*[1]

While this advice was well-meant, it didn't take into account various factors, such as the difficulty of growing food in areas with long, cold winters; the impossibility of growing major crops such as wheat and corn in a small plot of vacant land; and the fact that most Americans neither had experience growing food nor the money to buy important items such as seeds, fertilizer, and gardening equipment.

1. Henry Ford, "Ford, Self-Help, 1932," Hanover College History Department, accessed December 16, 2019, history.hanover.edu/courses/excerpts/336ford.html.

whether the American people … will maintain the spirit of charity and of mutual self-help … If we break down this sense of responsibility, of individual generosity to individual … we have not only [harmed] something infinitely valuable in the life of the American people but have struck at the roots of self-government … I am confident that our people have the resources, the initiative, the courage, the stamina and kindliness of spirit to meet this situation in the way they have met their problems over generations.[3]

Making Mistakes

Despite Hoover's traditional, conservative philosophy of government and economic affairs, he didn't think that his administration should sit back forever and watch the crisis unfold. He simply felt that the government should only do things that were appropriate for it to do. Years earlier, when he was helping European refugees and American flood victims, he had organized and coordinated relief efforts by businesses, charities, and government agencies. Faced with the major economic downturn that followed the crash of 1929, he employed the same approach. Late that year, the president summoned leading industrialists and government officials to the White House. He tried to persuade most of them, including wealthy car manufacturer Henry Ford, to consider not firing so many people and to not cut the wages of the employees they did keep. He also asked workers not to request raises. He believed all these measures would give Americans the ability to spend while not putting a strain on companies' profits, which could help fix the market. Hoover also spoke to the heads of the big utility companies about spending more on new construction projects. The hope was that this would create some much-needed job openings that anyone could fill.

In addition, Hoover devoted a significant amount of time and energy to organizing charity drives. During the winter of 1929 to 1930, he made numerous appeals to wealthy Americans, big companies, and religious institutions, asking them to donate money and goods to the poor. This effort produced some contributions, but they were a tiny amount relative to the scope of the national crisis. Around this same time, some congressmen urged the president to launch relief efforts funded by the federal government. He repeatedly refused to do so.

Hoover also declined proposals that the government create a large public works program to put people back to work; he didn't believe that taxpayer money should be spent on putting unemployed people on the federal government's payroll. Hoover and his advisers believed that a better way to repair the failing economy concerned tariffs. Tariffs are the taxes a company within the United States pays on imported goods. Generally, if tariffs increase, companies that use imported items also increase the cost the consumer, or buyer, has to pay. Hoover thought that, since the United States had such a large surplus of crops, raising tariffs on agricultural products would be a good way to encourage people to buy American crops instead of imported ones. The idea was to decrease the surplus and help struggling American farms. However, Congress also wanted to increase tariffs on other types of goods.

In June 1930, Hoover signed the Smoot-Hawley Tariff Act. Designed to encourage the production and sale of domestic products in the United States, the act raised America's already-high import tariffs on thousands of products. Hoover disagreed with this approach, but since the bill included higher agricultural tariffs, he felt that he had a duty to sign it. More than 1,000 economists saw the danger the Smoot-Hawley Act posed and signed a petition urging Hoover to veto the bill, but they were ignored. The results, as the economists had predicted, were disastrous. Many foreign nations retaliated by raising their own tariffs, which discouraged global trade. Between 1929 and 1932, imports fell by two-thirds and the revenue from American exports dropped by billions of dollars.

Another Hoover initiative, which ended up backfiring, was the Revenue Act of 1932. It was a huge tax increase across all income levels, largely in the form of income taxes. Hoover intended this new tax rate to increase federal revenues and balance the government's budget. However, these new taxes actually hurt the American economy: Because people now had much less money after paying these taxes, they were much less willing to spend it.

One of the federal programs the Revenue Act helped fund was the Reconstruction Finance Corporation (RFC), formed by Congress in 1932. The RFC's main function was to loan money to

Hoover and his advisers made many mistakes in their handling of the Great Depression. The country had never faced anything like this before, and its leaders were not able to quickly and effectively deal with problems like unemployment and factories that had to shut down.

failing banks, railroads, insurance companies, and other big businesses. The intention was to ensure that these institutions remained intact and didn't have to dissolve. That would, lawmakers hoped, create new jobs and maintain existing ones, thereby helping the economy. The RFC did save many businesses and was also helpful when it began loaning money to individual states in late 1932. This wasn't enough by itself, however, to significantly improve the devastated economy.

Sinking Deeper

The combined efforts of the Hoover administration to fight the Depression failed. Month by month, year by year, the country sank deeper and deeper into a financial pit. By 1933, more than 9,000 banks in the United States had failed and closed their doors. Because depositors had no insurance to back up their money, millions of Americans lost their entire life savings in less than a day.

American business and manufacturing losses during Hoover's term were also staggering. More than 26,000 businesses failed in 1930, and more than 28,000 did so in the year after. By 1932, the nation's volume of manufacturing was only 54 percent of what it had been before the 1929 market crash. The struggles of the rail industry were just one example of a previously profitable business suffering under the Depression. Going into the 1930s, railroads were still the most popular method of travel and shipping in America. As a result, large train corporations employed thousands of people. When the Depression hit, however, running a rail line became less profitable. People could barely even afford food, let alone travel, and for most of the Great Depression, railroad companies weren't profitable at all. An estimated one-third of America's rail companies went bankrupt in the 1930s. Tens of thousands of employees, who had believed they had a stable job in a successful industry, were laid off. Because of the banking failures, this left them with no money at all.

With millions of people losing their jobs as well as their savings, homelessness rose sharply in the early years of the Depression. Hundreds of thousands of families lost their homes during Hoover's years in office. All across America, the homeless gathered together and built small towns, where everyone lived in hand-built shacks in terrible conditions. Because so many people blamed Hoover's administration for the crisis, or at least for its failure to stop it, these areas where homeless people lived became known as "Hoovervilles."

Motivated by the worsening economic conditions in the country, some people staged public demonstrations to show the government their anger and frustration. Thousands of marches and rallies took place across the country during the Hoover years. These protests were sometimes broken up by force. In New York City, for instance, a large crowd was broken up by policemen who used violent

Hoovervilles such as this one were a common sight during the Great Depression.

methods. Demonstrations and protests were similarly broken up in Detroit, Michigan; Cleveland, Ohio; and Boston, Massachusetts.

The most notorious use of violence against demonstrators came only a few years after the onset of the Depression. During the summer of 1932, around 15,000 World War I veterans marched on Washington, DC, to demand that the government pay them bonus money that they had been promised but had not yet received. These men camped out near the Capitol in tents and makeshift shelters, waiting for Congress or the president to act. This group was commonly called the "Bonus Army" because they were fighting for their bonus. Most of the protestors needed that bonus money to survive. Though a large number of frustrated men made up the Bonus Army, its leader, Walter W. Waters, was able to keep their demonstration largely peaceful. After Congress voted down a bill that would allow them to collect their bonuses, most of the protestors went home. The few thousand who remained demonstrated more aggressively, so the US armed forces were sent in. Soldiers drove the veterans away with tear gas and then set fire to their shelters. The crackdown wounded and killed several protestors and police officers.

HISTORY HAPPENED HERE: HOOVERVILLES

As the Great Depression wore on and homelessness worsened, Hoovervilles began to pop up across the country. The number of unemployed and homeless was so large that these nearly became towns in their own right. According to History.com, by 1935, the largest Hooverville—located in St. Louis, Missouri—had its own mayor, separate neighborhoods, and four churches, at least one of which was built out of orange crates. The website also described life in a typical Hooverville:

> *Whenever possible, Hoovervilles were built near rivers for the convenience of a water source ... Some Hoovervilles were dotted with vegetable gardens, and some individual shacks contained furniture a family had managed to carry away upon eviction from their former home. However, Hoovervilles were typically grim and unsanitary. They posed health risks to their inhabitants as well as to those living nearby, but there was little that local governments or health agencies could do. Hooverville residents had nowhere to go, and public sympathy, for the most part, was with them.*[1]

Most Hoovervilles were torn down during or after the Depression. However, during the Great Recession, similar institutions cropped up again as a result of economic hardship that resulted in an increased rate of homelessness. Instead of being called Hoovervilles, these are generally known as "tent cities," but the principle is the same. Every state as well as the District of Columbia has reported at least one tent city, but it's hard to get an accurate count of people living in them because most are illegal. In contrast to Hoovervilles, most communities don't tolerate tent cities, and governments often raid them to kick out or arrest the people living there.

1. "Hoovervilles," History.com, modified November 2, 2018, www.history.com/topics/great-depression/hoovervilles.

These violent government reactions to discontent didn't improve the national mood, and the spreading public opinion was that Hoover and his administration had to go. Historically, it's clear that the president didn't cause the Depression. The unwise economic practices of the 1920s were the primary culprit. However, a bad situation grew worse on Hoover's watch, so many people ended up blaming him for the entire crisis.

A New Leader

Faced with the continuing disaster of the Great Depression, the Republican Party, which was in power at the time, worried about the next presidential election. After all, Hoover was widely hated throughout the country for his ineffective policies—millions of people had lost their jobs and savings while he was in charge, and the country was in the midst of its worst economic period ever—and there were no signs that things were going to get better. People were rapidly losing faith in the Republican Party.

Franklin Delano Roosevelt won voters' trust by promising to focus his energy on fixing the economy.

It had been historically difficult to get elected over a president who was currently in office, but Franklin Delano Roosevelt (often called FDR), the Democratic Party's nominee, believed he could win thanks to this decreased support for Republicans in general and for Hoover in particular. Roosevelt knew the most important issue in America was fixing the economy, and he pledged to focus almost entirely on doing so. In his acceptance speech at the Democratic Convention, he said,

> *What do the people of America want more than anything else? To my mind, they want two things: work, with all the moral and spiritual values that go with it; and with work, a reasonable measure of security—security for themselves and for their wives and children … I pledge you, I pledge myself, to a new deal for the American people. Let us all here assembled constitute ourselves prophets of a new order of competence and of courage. This is more than a political campaign; it is a call to arms. Give me your help, not to win votes alone, but to win in this crusade to restore America to its own people.*[4]

Roosevelt had specific ideas for a path to financial recovery, and his political track record was positive: He was the highly successful governor of New York from 1929 to 1932. On Election Day in 1932, he won the presidency by a wide margin. He quickly started instituting new programs, policies, and reforms, which collectively became known as the New Deal. The first three months of his term were immediately successful in stimulating the economy and restoring the public's faith in the presidency.

Roosevelt's Goals

Part of the reason Roosevelt was able to make so many significant changes was that he was a skilled leader, speaker, and communicator, with many years of political experience. He had been born into a wealthy family, and he had a strong desire to use his personal gifts and privileged position to serve the public. He served as a New York State senator from 1911 to 1913, and he was an assistant secretary of the US Navy during World War I. Not long after the war, Roosevelt got sick. For decades, historians believed the disease he contracted was polio, although a 2003 study in the *Journal of Medical Biography* suggested that his symptoms more closely matched those of the neurological disease Guillain-Barré syndrome. However, the specific disease is less important than the outcome: Roosevelt lost his ability to walk. Despite this setback, he reentered politics, serving as governor of New York during Hoover's presidential term. His policies during this time won him widespread affection across the state.

Running against Hoover, Roosevelt consistently used the awful economic and social conditions of the Depression against the Republicans. He said the government needed to do more to alleviate the crisis and to repair the broken economy. He reached out to the poor and jobless, members of organized labor unions, and people of color, trying to forge a widespread and diverse voter base that would elect him.

This strategy worked phenomenally. In November 1932, Roosevelt won by a landslide, getting 472 electoral votes to Hoover's 59. The Democrats also secured a majority control of both houses of Congress, winning the House 310 to 117 and the Senate 60 to 35. Roosevelt's administration took these signs as a message from the American people: The new president needed to do whatever it took to end the Depression.

Roosevelt hinted at how broad his plan was in his inaugural address, delivered on March 4, 1933. This speech was remarkable for a number of reasons, especially at the time. Instead of making empty political promises, such as telling everyone in America that he could immediately solve every economic issue, he said that it was going to be a long, difficult path to recovery. Moreover, he said that before the United States could enact political and economic change, its people must adopt a major attitude change: They must face and conquer the state of fear that currently gripped the country.

Reactions to Roosevelt's speech were universally favorable. After years of what many perceived as governmental inaction, a mood of active optimism began to spread across the nation. The American humorist and political commentator Will Rogers captured that mood when he stated:

> *America hasn't been so happy in three years as they are today. No money, no banks, no work, no nothing, but they know they got a man in there who is wise to Congress, wise to our big bankers,*

and wise to our so-called big men. The whole country is with him even if what he does is wrong. They are with him, just so he does something. If he burned down the Capitol we would cheer and say, "Well, we at least got a fire started, anyhow."[5]

Roosevelt and his advisers knew they had a lot of work to do to earn the people's trust, but what exactly should they do? The truth was that the country's economic crisis was so huge and serious that no one, not even the finest economists of the time, knew how to begin fixing it. As a result, the new administration launched a bold, broad attack on the Depression. Officials initiated multiple government-run programs, most of which were experimental, hoping that at least some would work. This was the exact opposite of Hoover's conservative approach, in which government played a minimal role.

Addressing the Currency Problem

The first major move Roosevelt's government made was an attempt to stabilize the value of US currency, which had been declining, as a way to restore confidence in America's banks. On March 6, 1933, not even two full days after he had taken office, the president called a special session of Congress and suggested a national bank holiday. This meant that all the nation's banks would close down until March 10, 1933, to allow accountants from the US Treasury time to inspect their records and transactions. This would reveal which banks were most in need of emergency government aid. After that, only the banks whose finances were in good shape would be allowed to reopen. This would prevent more banks from failing and losing customers' savings.

Though this was a daring and unprecedented move, most congressmen, senators, and bankers felt it was necessary. The House of Representatives swiftly approved the bank holiday bill, and a few hours later the Senate passed it nearly unanimously. Only seven hours after submitting the bill to Congress, Roosevelt signed it into law. It was the fastest passage of a piece of federal legislation in US history.

Roosevelt realized that national legislators weren't the only people whose support he needed to make the bank holiday a success. It was important for ordinary citizens, on whose financial deposits banks depended, to understand what was happening. To explain his strategy, the president held his first "fireside chat" on March 12, 1933. Repeated throughout his presidency, fireside chats were radio addresses in which he outlined national problems and challenges as well as explained or defended government policies. In an era before the internet or television, this was an effective way

FDR's fireside chats not only gave Americans important information, they also improved morale by strengthening the public's trust in their leader.

to give everyone in the country the same news in a timely manner. In his broadcasts, Roosevelt spoke plainly, as if he were talking to a friend rather than making a speech. In his first broadcast, he said:

> *Why are all the banks not to be reopened at the same time? The answer is simple and I know you will understand it: Your Government does not intend that the history of the past few years shall be repeated. We do not want and will not have another epidemic of bank failures.*
>
> *As a result, we start tomorrow, Monday, with the opening of the banks … which on first examination by the Treasury, have already been found to be all right … [Later, banks] all through the country will resume business … Please let me make it clear to you that if your bank does not open the first day you are by no means justified in believing it will not open.*[6]

The broadcast helped millions of Americans understand and benefit from the sweeping bank closures and reopenings. The new administration quickly ended the worst of the national banking crisis and restored public confidence in the country's banks.

Relief Acts

Roosevelt wasn't content to simply pass a few laws, however. Instead, he wanted to completely reorganize and revolutionize the federal government. To do so, he pushed through a startling amount of bills and policies. The number and magnitude of the federal programs he introduced in his first hundred days in office easily exceeded what some previous presidents had accomplished in their entire four-year terms.

In March 1933, the same month in which he declared the bank holiday, Roosevelt called for the creation of a major new aid program. This organization was named the Civilian Conservation Corps (CCC). Run by the military, its primary function was to provide work for the hundreds of thousands of young men who were unemployed. They would be put to work planting trees, fighting forest fires, digging ditches, creating trails in national parks, and other jobs involving manual labor that any healthy man could do. The CCC gave more than 3 million young men jobs from 1933 to 1942. This not only reduced the unemployment rate, but also increased the amount of money being spent by civilians in the economy: The CCC men kept some of their salary, but they sent most of the money they earned back to their families. Most importantly, the program helped the young men who worked for it survive. It was far from the only government-sponsored program in the 1930s to do so.

The Agricultural Adjustment Act (AAA), passed in May 1933, was a bold and controversial piece of legislation. It created the Agricultural Adjustment Administration, whose purpose was to increase poor farmers' profits by temporarily paying them to produce less grain, corn, rice, livestock, and other items. The hope was that,

Shown here are CCC men planting new trees on an Oregon hillside that had been clear-cut.

PAST MEETS PRESENT: AMERICORPS NCCC

In 1993, President Bill Clinton signed the National and Community Service Trust Act. One of the things this act did was create a federal volunteer program called AmeriCorps. AmeriCorps has many branches, but the National Civilian Community Corps (NCCC) in particular was modeled after the CCC. People who sign up for AmeriCorps NCCC are assigned to one of four home bases and spend 10 months traveling to states around that base, doing community service projects. Like the original CCC, these often include environmental work, but they can also include things such as building houses or working with children.

While the CCC was intended to put unemployed men to work, AmeriCorps NCCC is a volunteer program, which means the participants receive very little money for their work. People join largely because they want to help others. However, in 1997, the AmeriCorps Education Award was established as a way to reward AmeriCorps volunteers by helping them go to college or pay off old student loans.

AmeriCorps volunteers participate in a wide range of projects, including working in schools and community centers.

as these commodities became less common, they would be worth more. This would lead to a price increase for agricultural goods, and farmers' wages would increase as well. At that time, they would no longer need the government subsidy, or payment.

Initial reactions to the AAA were mixed. Economists saw the wisdom of the plan, and farmers were happy to make more money. Many ordinary Americans, however, objected to the idea of producing less food at a time when many people were starving. They especially disliked it when AAA officials ordered that millions of farm animals be slaughtered and thousands of acres of cotton be destroyed, which would help raise prices and profits for farmers. However, as Robert S. McElvaine noted, "The AAA concept of limiting production was no more [illogical] than the economic system itself, which found no way to bring together idle [unused] workers and idle factories or hungry people and unsold crops."[7]

Roosevelt also created the Federal Emergency Relief Administration (FERA), organized in May 1933. He appointed his friend and adviser, Harry Hopkins, director of this important new agency. FERA was designed to reduce unemployment. It distributed funds to individual states, allowing them to establish and run local work projects. After just two years, FERA was disbanded and replaced with the Works Progress Administration (WPA), but in that time, it provided jobs to more than 20 million Americans who had been out of work.

Still another of Roosevelt's daring and effective programs was the Tennessee Valley Authority (TVA), also created in May 1933. One of the largest construction projects in world history, it aimed to construct a series of huge dams in the Tennessee River Valley. The structures, Roosevelt claimed, would give millions of Americans cheap electricity, help control damaging floods that occurred almost every year in the area, and provide years of work for tens of thousands of people. The TVA was an overwhelming success, accomplishing all of the goals Roosevelt said it would.

Giving People Hope

Though they're the most well-known, the CCC, AAA, FERA, and TVA weren't the only important programs the Roosevelt administration introduced in the historic Hundred Days—his first 100 days as president. Some of the others included the Economy Act, which was intended to reduce the size of the federal government; the Securities Act, which was organized to reform the stock market and make future crashes less likely; and the Home Owners Loan Act, which would help low-income families get mortgages so they could buy homes.

As these comprehensive programs started to roll out, the American people started to regain confidence in the future. The general view was that even if some of these programs didn't work, at least the government was making a real effort to turn things around. Though some conservative observers criticized the growing role of the government, most people were simply happy to have food and shelter.

Moreover, the American people weren't the only ones closely watching the way Roosevelt was fighting the Depression. Many other countries were experiencing the same dramatic financial slump. They hoped that America's ongoing economic and political experiments would be successful; if they were, their effects would ripple outward and help everyone.

How You See History

1. Was it right for people to blame Hoover for the Depression?
2. Why did FDR's policies seem to work better than Hoover's?
3. What policies might you create if you were trying to fix the Great Depression?

CHAPTER THREE

HELPING A NATION RECOVER

Roosevelt's first hundred days in office were unusually busy, and he didn't stop when they were over. He continued putting policies in place to help the nation recover and help individuals survive the tough times. However, he didn't do it alone. Though Roosevelt himself was an intelligent, creative, and qualified individual, his presidential terms were supported by a group of men nicknamed the "Brain Trust" by journalist John F. Kieran. This term spread rapidly, and most Americans associated Roosevelt's success with the members of the Brain Trust. The most prominent members of this group were Rexford G. Tugwell, Adolf A. Berle Jr., and Raymond Moley, all three of whom were professors at Columbia University—one of the top schools in the country. They advised Roosevelt in a range of political fields, from economic issues to social problems.

Critics of the Brain Trust accused its members of being idealistic, irresponsible spenders and of being disconnected from the problems they were trying to solve. However, though their programs were certainly not all successful, they kept trying and didn't let setbacks stop them. The programs and institutions they suggested were often unique, creative, and bold ways of addressing the nation's massive economic problems. Any new idea that seemed promising was given a chance to succeed. The New Deal era was a time of

Members of Roosevelt's "Brain Trust," such as Rex Tugwell (*left*), could often be seen with him as he carried out official government business.

experimentation; because no one had ever seen an economic crisis similar to the Depression, the Brain Trust and FDR believed that they also needed solutions that had never been seen before.

Taking Risks

The new programs created by Roosevelt's administration ranged from resounding successes to mediocre failures. None of his initiatives were truly catastrophic, and many were extraordinarily helpful for millions of Americans. Roosevelt knew he was taking a political risk by creating unique programs, but that was part of his strategy. Gardiner C. Means, who held high positions in several New Deal agencies, later said, "It was … experimentation that made the New Deal what it was. A hundred years from now, when historians look back on it, they will say a big corner was turned. People agreed that old things didn't work. What ran through the whole New Deal was finding a way to make things work."[1] The approach of remaking the nation through trial and error was a big part of the spirit of the New Deal and of the times. It certainly worked effectively to lower unemployment and stimulate the economy, but it was nonetheless a major gamble.

Roosevelt's grand experiment in fighting the Depression, reorganizing the economy, and changing society paid off—both for him and the country. He was able to lead the United States through the Great Depression and through most of World War II. Some of his programs, however, have been criticized over time, and conservative Republicans believed that the government was getting too big. Critics also believed that Roosevelt was too willing to experiment and try new things; some voters saw this as a sign that he lacked the ability to follow through on plans that had already been put in motion.

Giving Help Where It Was Needed

Critiques of Roosevelt's ability to complete his big ideas were both right and wrong. It's true that a number of Roosevelt's New Deal programs did close down after only a few years of operation. However, some lasted for more than a decade, and some were so enormously successful that as of 2020, they're still in operation. One example of

This diagram explains how the TVA used a series of dams to meet residents' electricity needs and keep them safe from flooding.

this is the TVA, which still provides power to millions of Americans. Another is Social Security, which is one of the most prominent social fixtures in the country.

The goal of the Social Security Act, implemented in August 1935, was to help citizens who were in particular need because of old age, job loss, or some kind of disability. Today, as it was back then, both employers and employees contribute to a special Social Security fund. The Social Security Administration (SSA) then distributes the money to people who are older than 65, temporarily unemployed, or physically unable to work. When people talk about Social Security today, they generally mean the insurance for people who are retired; however, according to USA.gov, the four main types of benefits the SSA offers are retirement benefits, disability benefits, benefits for survivors of income-earning family members who have died, and Supplemental Security Income (SSI). SSI covers people who are over 65 or disabled and who have limited income or resources, such as a car or house. For example, a person who is deaf, doesn't own a car, and makes less than $2,000 per month would likely be eligible for SSI.

Just as it is a widely debated political topic today, Social Security was a controversial initiative when Roosevelt and his advisers proposed it. Many people, especially conservatives, argued against it because it entailed the government giving people money they had not directly earned. They worried that this was potentially harmful because they thought it might promote laziness or reward people for not working. James L. Donnelly, former spokesman for the Illinois Manufacturers' Association, warned that Social Security would undermine American life and American values "by destroying initiative, discouraging thrift [wise spending and saving], and stifling individual responsibility."[2]

Roosevelt and the many Americans who supported the idea of Social Security countered by pointing out that the new system did not simply give people free money. Every person who ever did any sort of work would pay a little into the system by having a small tax taken out of their paycheck. Therefore, they would contribute to their own retirement or unemployment insurance. Moreover,

Posters such as this one were displayed in post offices and other public areas in the 1930s. Today, American citizens are assigned a Social Security number at birth. This number is needed to get a job, driver's license, and many other necessities.

HISTORY HAPPENED HERE: CCC PROJECTS

Most CCC projects involved things such as building trails and national parks, and many of these are maintained today. These include:

- Manistee National Forest in Michigan
- Florida Caverns State Park in Florida
- Balmorhea State Park in Texas
- Zion National Park in Utah
- Timberline Lodge in Oregon

The camps where the men lived are now gone, but in some places, plaques mark the spot where they once stood.

The CCC built Timberline Lodge on Mt. Hood in Oregon. In 1980, it was used as the exterior of the fictional Overlook Hotel in *The Shining*, the classic film adaptation of Stephen King's novel.

economists argued that the program was a wise way to help guard against future depressions and mass poverty.

Today, people still debate the positive and negative aspects of the Social Security Act. While it has unquestionably not led to the downfall of a working society, some people believe the program is too easily abused and should be restricted or abolished completely. Others argue that the stories of abuse are exaggerated and that getting rid of it would make it difficult or impossible for a large segment of society to survive.

The New Deal Pays Off

Some of the most successful New Deal initiatives were created with the primary goal of putting the millions of unemployed Americans back to work. In this regard, the CCC was a hallmark program. A 1936 poll taken by Gallup, a data collection and analysis corporation, found that 82 percent of Americans were strongly in favor of the CCC because it found decent-paying work for millions of young men. The program lasted roughly nine years, and at its height, it employed 500,000 men simultaneously. Though it closed down in 1942, it likely would've remained active had the United States not entered World War II. After the country began fighting, most of the young men who would've found jobs through the CCC joined the military instead.

Another large portion of Americans managed to find employment through the Public Works Administration (PWA). This popular program was headed by Secretary of the Interior Harold L. Ickes. Known for his honesty, organizational skills, and work ethic, Ickes was one of the leading figures of the New Deal and a major player in the US government from 1933 to 1946. Under his guidance, the PWA made deals with private contractors to construct buildings, highways, and other public works projects. Their goal was to both employ as many citizens as possible and improve the infrastructure of the country.

The sheer scope of the PWA's accomplishments was huge. Between 1933 and 1939, it spent $4 billion to employ Americans to build more than 34,000 streets, highways, schools, dams, airports, hospitals, sewage systems, tunnels, and navy warships. Among the best-known public works the agency created are New

THEY MADE HISTORY: HAROLD L. ICKES

Harold L. Ickes was one of the leading US government officials in the 1930s and 1940s and a major contributor to the New Deal during the Depression era. Born in Pennsylvania in 1874, he was a social activist and lawyer. In his early life, he provided legal representation for clients suing for civil liberties—often at no charge. Soon, he became a Republican political operative, supporting the policies of FDR's cousin, President Theodore Roosevelt. In 1933, FDR—a Democrat who wanted a Republican in his cabinet for the sake of political balance—asked Ickes to serve as secretary of the interior. In this position, he is most remembered for defending natural resources against corporate exploitation. Ickes also served as director of the Public Works Administration, where he distributed billions of dollars to give unemployed Americans jobs. Ickes was a powerful champion of civil liberties and civil rights. He also openly criticized the government's internment of Japanese Americans during World War II. Ickes resigned from the government in 1946 after an argument with President Harry S. Truman. He died in Washington, DC, in 1952.

York City's Lincoln Tunnel, Washington State's Grand Coulee Dam, and the Overseas Highway connecting Key West, Florida, to the US mainland.

Even more widespread than the PWA was another New Deal program designed to put people to work: the Works Progress Administration (WPA). Created in 1935, the WPA was headed by Harry Hopkins, who also directed FERA. The WPA was the largest New Deal program by a significant margin. From 1935 to 1943, 8.5 million Americans in a wide range of professions were employed by the WPA. Like the other New Deal initiatives, the WPA funded the building of roads, bridges, and airport runways, which were critical pieces of infrastructure. The WPA also built libraries, city halls, and parks, and it devoted 7 percent of its budget to funding arts-related projects. Among the subprograms of the WPA were the Federal Writers' Project, the Federal Theatre Project, and the Federal Music Project. These and other similar programs helped America's artists and authors find an outlet for their creative talents. They were a vital part of keeping hope alive through the difficult Depression years.

Reforming Business

Most of these large-scale employment programs put in place during the New Deal were designed to create new jobs, which would allow the millions of unemployed Americans to earn money. Some of this money would be spent, and this would stimulate the depressed economy. Meanwhile, millions of other Americans had been fortunate enough to keep their jobs in existing industries and businesses, but many others who had specific skills in these industries had recently been laid off. Many big employers had cut back, partly because their businesses were disorganized, not working to capacity, and not taking advantage of their workers.

In an effort to make American industry more efficient and fair, which would lead to expansion and the creation of more jobs, Congress passed the National Industrial Recovery Act (NIRA) in 1933. This act created the National Recovery Administration (NRA), headed by Hugh S. Johnson, a retired military general and a member of Roosevelt's Brain Trust. The NRA was designed to help factories and other large businesses plan for the future; to restore competition in the market, which had diminished along with the suffering economy; to regulate prices so industries couldn't unfairly overcharge consumers; to set the number of hours employees could work each week, which would reduce exploitation of the workers; and to eliminate child labor.

The goals set by the NRA were broad, diverse, and affected tens of millions of employers and employees across all levels of society. Collecting reliable data from hundreds of thousands of businesses across the country was a monumental undertaking—and, in an era before digital records, difficult for researchers to access. For this

PAST MEETS PRESENT: THE GREEN NEW DEAL

Inspired by the reforms of the New Deal, Representative Alexandria Ocasio-Cortez and Senator Ed Markey released a plan in February 2019 called the Green New Deal. "Green" refers to the fact that one of the major goals of the plan is to address climate change, but it also includes reforms of the social safety net that the original New Deal put into place. Some of the Green New Deal's aims include:

- meeting 100 percent of American energy demands through renewable sources of power
- making all buildings in the United States energy efficient
- cutting carbon emissions from all forms of transportation, including buses, cars, and airplanes
- guaranteeing all Americans a job with paid vacation time, a retirement plan, and a salary that can support a family
- high-quality medical care for all Americans
- stronger labor laws that protect all workers
- better access to a college education for all students
- honoring treaties with Native Americans and getting their permission before building anything on land they own

As of early 2020, the Green New Deal has not been officially adopted by the government. Furthermore, Ocasio-Cortez and Markey haven't explained exactly how they plan to achieve the ambitious goals laid out in their plan. As with Roosevelt, a lot of it may very well end up being trial and error, with some plans succeeding and others failing. Again, as with Roosevelt, critics have complained that the plan will cost a lot of money and represents government overreach. Only time will tell whether the Green New Deal will be as successful as the original New Deal.

reason, it's unclear how successful each aspect of the program was and how much it actually helped the economy. Most historians agree that, even though the NRA didn't single-handedly lift the country out of the Depression in the 1930s, it was a crucial component of the country's long-term economic stability. In addition to making important changes in the way businesses were run, the NRA "changed the attitudes of business and the public. It revived belief that something [positive] could be done."[3]

Two other crucial bills passed in 1933 were the Banking Act and the Glass-Steagall Act, which together created the Federal Deposit Insurance Corporation (FDIC). Roosevelt knew that people had lost faith in banks after they had lost their savings, so a main role of the FDIC was to insure customers' money. Most customers today are insured up to $250,000. This means that if your bank fails tomorrow, the FDIC will give you the amount of money you had in your accounts up to $250,000. The FDIC also teaches people about banks, answers complaints, and provides oversight to make sure banks are acting within the law and not taking risks such as the ones that led to the Great Depression.

At first, the American Bankers Association opposed the FDIC, believing it was too expensive and wouldn't be truly helpful at reforming the banks. However, when only nine banks closed the year after it was passed, people saw the value of the organization. The FDIC further proved its worth in 1988—the first year after World

Banks that are insured by the FDIC often display a sign similar to this one.

War II that the organization actually had to pay customers their deposit insurance. Changing laws led to the deregulation of banks, which, in turn, allowed banks to start taking economic risks again. Just as in the Great Depression, this led to bank failures, but another depression was averted by the existence of the FDIC and its insurance policy, which is still in place today.

Dealing with Failures

Despite its many successes, an experiment as bold, widespread, and unique as the New Deal was bound to produce at least a few failed initiatives. One example was its attempt to change the Supreme Court. Toward the end of his first term, the Court began declaring

FROM THE SOURCE: A FIRESIDE CHAT

In a fireside chat broadcast on March 9, 1937, Roosevelt told the American people:

> *In the last four years ... the [Supreme] Court has been acting not, as a judicial body, but as a policymaking body ... The Court ... has improperly set itself up as a third House of the Congress—a superlegislature, as one of the justices has called it—reading into the Constitution words and implications which are not there and which were never intended to be there.*
>
> *We have, therefore, reached the point as a nation where we must take action to save the Constitution from the Court and the Court from itself. We must find a way to take an appeal from the Supreme Court to the Constitution itself. We want a Supreme Court which will do justice under the Constitution—not over it.*[1]

1. Quoted in "'Younger and More Vigorous Blood': FDR on the Judiciary," History Matters, accessed January 7, 2020, historymatters.gmu.edu/d/5092.

some of Roosevelt's progressive programs illegal or unconstitutional. The president and most of his advisers thought that these decisions were the result of too many old, conservative judges on the court—men who were old-fashioned and suspicious of new, liberal ideas.

Roosevelt attempted to work around the Supreme Court by introducing the Judicial Procedures Reform Bill of 1937, also known as the "court-packing" bill. Its main purpose was to give the president the right to appoint an extra Supreme Court justice for each existing judge who was older than 70. Each of these extra judges would be handpicked for their loyalty to Roosevelt and his New Deal. Considering the configuration of the Court at the time, this would have expanded it by an extra six justices, and it would have ensured that most or all of Roosevelt's programs would be approved.

The bill raised protests from both Republicans and Democrats. Opponents worried that it would give the office of president too much authority and create an imbalance of power among the executive, legislative, and judicial branches of government. Accordingly, the Senate rejected the idea almost immediately. However, for reasons that are still debated by historians, the Court began to vote more often in Roosevelt's favor after this bill was defeated. As a result, most elements of the New Deal remained in place throughout Roosevelt's presidency.

How You See History

1. Do you think Social Security is still necessary today? Explain your answer.
2. Would you have joined the CCC during the Depression? Why do you think people join programs such as AmeriCorps today? Explain your answers.
3. How do you think Roosevelt's policies might have been different without the input of his Brain Trust?

CHAPTER FOUR

LIVING THROUGH THE DEPRESSION

Living through the Great Depression was a daily struggle for most people. People saved everything they got and tried to make it last as long as they could, and for many people, this pattern of behavior lasted the rest of their lives—even after the economy picked up again. Food was scarce, and Depression recipes such as "tomato soup" (ketchup mixed with warm water) and "cooked bread" (stale bread covered in olive oil, salt, and boiling water to make it soft enough to eat) became widespread.

In addition to difficulty affording food, people often suffered from inadequate clothing and shelter. In 1932, investigative reporter Lorena A. Hickok wrote this description of how people endured a Midwestern winter:

> *Last Winter the temperature went down to 40 degrees below zero and stayed there ten days, while a 60-mile [per hour] wind howled across the plains. And entering that kind of a Winter we have between 4,000 and 5,000 human beings … without clothing or bedding, getting just enough food to keep them from starving. No fuel. Living in houses that a prosperous farmer wouldn't put his cattle in.*[1]

Poverty was widespread during the Great Depression. People could barely afford food and clothing, let alone things such as new appliances or home repairs.

In cities, people were not living much differently. Thousands ended up homeless and hungry. Hundreds of thousands of people waited for hours—sometimes all day—in bread lines because they simply had no other way to access food.

However, despite all of this hardship, life went on. People took joy where they could; for example, many families already owned radios and would gather together at night to listen to entertainment programs, the way families watch TV together today. Other free activities included playing sports in a park, entering a contest such as a dance marathon, or playing board games. Sometimes people would treat themselves to an inexpensive activity such as going to a baseball game or a movie. Times were hard for everyone, but some people had it harder than others.

Looking for Work

One of the worst aspects of the Depression for many people was unemployment. The economy simply couldn't support enough jobs for everyone after the stock market crash of 1929, and there had been little improvement during Hoover's presidency. Few jobs were available before Roosevelt's New Deal programs began putting people back to work. As successful as these programs were, they didn't completely solve the terrible unemployment epidemic. In 1935, for example, the unemployment rate was still 20 percent, and as late as 1940, it remained high at 14.5 percent. For comparison, experts consider an unemployment rate of between 4 and 6 percent to be a sign of a healthy economy.

The task of job-hunting, therefore, became one of the focal points of Depression life in towns and cities across the United States—even though job seekers knew they wouldn't find anything. The reason for this fanatical search was ingrained in the American spirit: People who were unemployed were often considered lazy and a drain on society. The fact that 20 percent of Americans were suddenly unemployed through no fault of their own couldn't change this stubborn belief. Robert S. McElvaine explained:

> *A widespread attitude of the unemployed early in the Depression was: "There must be something wrong with a [man] who can't get*

a job.” Sure, I’ve lost my job, but I’m still a worthy provider. Work will turn up soon *[they would think]. Every morning up before dawn, washed, shaved, and dressed as neatly as possible. To the factory gates, only to find a hundred others already there, staring blankly at the sign: NO HELP WANTED. The search then became more feverish.*[2]

This attitude was reinforced by the people who still had jobs. Rather than considering themselves lucky, many falsely saw

Being out of work took a psychological as well as a financial toll on many men. Shown here are two men attaching signs to their car advertising their desire to work and assuring others that they aren’t lazy, as many people thought unemployed men were.

themselves as somehow naturally better than the people who had lost their jobs. People seeking employment and asking for food were frequently called insulting names and dismissed as people who were only looking for handouts instead of working for themselves. Of course, since these people were trying desperately to find work to support themselves and their families, this was a misconception.

The worst part of these verbal torments was the undeniable psychological impact they carried. Most American men were used to being breadwinners—providers who worked to give their families a good life—and they didn't know what it meant to be unemployed. They felt bad enough about themselves already, and hearing the names people called them often reinforced those feelings. Joseph L. Heffernan, mayor of Youngstown, Ohio, during the Depression's early years, recalled, "One man I had known for years stood at my desk and calmly said, 'My wife is frantic. After working at the steel mill for twenty-five years, I have lost my job, and I'm too old to get other work. If you can't do something for me, I'm going to kill myself.'"[3] Mayor Heffernan was able to secure this particular man a job, so he didn't end up taking his own life; many others weren't so lucky.

The psychological effects of long-term unemployment could be deadly. America's national suicide rate rose from 12 per 100,000 in 1929 to more than 17 per 100,000 in 1932. This was a jump of almost 50 percent. The rate was even higher in many cities that had been hit particularly hard by the Depression. At the time, mental health care was much more stigmatized, or seen negatively, than it is today. Men, especially, generally considered asking for help or seeing a therapist to be a sign of weakness. Even if this stigma hadn't existed, though, finding the money to seek help would have been difficult or impossible.

Effects on the Family

Widespread unemployment and poverty also disrupted traditional family roles in communities all across the country. The typical status and responsibilities of men, women, and children in these families changed, sometimes dramatically. In particular, the status of the man as the primary breadwinner and head of the family diminished. Before the Depression, a man generally made the rules at home because his job supported the family. When he could no longer provide for them, society began to experience some changes. If a man couldn't reliably make money, people began questioning why he was the leader of the family.

In addition, many men found themselves stuck hanging around the house. They were intruding into what had traditionally been the woman's sphere. One positive result of this trend was that some men learned to see things more from a woman's perspective. In many families, however, men being stuck in the house all day had negative consequences. Some couples, together all day and all night and suffering from poverty, unemployment, and hunger, were more likely to get into arguments. In some cases, a husband was unable to find work, but other members of his immediate family were able to secure a job. This could damage a man's pride and make him more likely to lash out violently at relatives. Though divorce rates during the Depression decreased, some historians claim that this was because people couldn't afford the legal fees of a divorce, since reports also indicate that the rate of marriage desertion (simply walking away from one's spouse without filing for divorce) increased in the 1930s.

Even in cases where parents stayed together, children suffered as well. Parents under stress tried to hide their worries from their children, but sometimes they simply couldn't. As one man from Arizona said, "Sometimes you would look at your children and wonder what would happen to them … Often you cry like a youngster; you try to do it privately, but you know the children hear you."[4]

Only the most fortunate children were able to remain in school. Because of financial disaster, numerous towns and cities across the nation were forced to close some of their public schools. Some children had to quit attending a school that remained open to help their parents make ends meet. Young boys worked in fields or helped repair aging and failing family vehicles. Young girls helped their mothers make or mend clothes and looked after younger siblings. Nationwide, more than 3 million children between the ages of 7

Children weren't sheltered from the realities of the Depression. Child labor was newly outlawed, but many still had to quit school to help their families.

and 17 had left school by the 1930s. Some of them managed to find work outside the home through the CCC, but many who quit school remained jobless for years.

Looking for an Escape

Whether someone had a job during the Depression or not, surviving from one week to the next was life's major priority. No matter how hard things got, though, people made time for fun whenever they could. In fact, Americans pursued a wide range of leisure and entertainment activities all throughout the 1930s. Sporting events, holiday parades and picnics, high school band concerts, community dances, county fairs, and traveling carnivals were all free or cheap forms of entertainment.

Despite the hard economic times, movies flourished during the Great Depression. For millions of Americans, watching films was a way to escape from the bleak reality of their lives. Between 60 million and 70 million people—roughly 50 percent of the entire population of the United States—attended a movie at least once a week during the 1930s. The main reason so many people could afford it was that tickets were inexpensive. On average, admission cost about 10 cents for children and 20 cents for adults—the equivalent of between $1 and $4 today. Moviegoers got a lot for their money, as well; included in a single ticket price, most theaters ran two full-length movies, one or two shorter cartoons, and a short newsreel summarizing the national and world events of the past week.

Depression-era Americans were also drawn to movie theaters by the specific subject matter of films. For the most part, films set in reality or depicting life realistically weren't popular in the 1930s. These films reminded people of the harsh world they had to return to after leaving the theater, which defeated the entire purpose of attending a movie. Instead, most moviegoers preferred to be transported into over-the-top or fantasy worlds. Musicals such as *42nd Street* and *The Gold Diggers* were widely popular, as were Westerns. Because the movie industry was relatively prosperous during the Depression, movie quality generally increased. Some films released in the 1930s, such as *Gone With the Wind*, are still famous and beloved

In the 1930s, families would gather around their radio in the evening the way families today often watch TV together.

by people today.

Another popular activity during the Great Depression was listening to the radio. People most frequently tuned in for music and news, but because television hadn't been invented yet, people could also listen to radio sitcoms, dramas, mysteries, detective shows, and other episodic programs similar to those later seen on TV. In fact, a number of popular radio shows, such as comedian Jack Benny's sitcom, became popular television programs in the 1950s. One of the most popular radio programs of the 1930s was *Amos 'n' Andy*, a nightly comedy about two friends who regularly found themselves in humorous situations. More than 40 million people—roughly one-third of all Americans—listened to the show each night in 1931.

Listening to the radio was free, but in an era in which money was scarce, many people tried to combine money-making with their leisure activities. Gambling games such as blackjack were extremely popular, and people also liked to bet on the outcomes of pinball games, as pinball machines became hugely popular after they were first introduced in the United States in the early 1930s.

Another way people tried to have fun and strike it rich at the same time was by participating in competitions. One of the most popular types of competitions were called dance marathons. As the name implies, these were public competitions in which couples started dancing at a certain time and continued as long as they could. The couple who danced the longest would win a cash prize. However, some of these marathons could last for several weeks straight—the longest lasted for almost six months—so by the end, contestants were too exhausted to truly dance. Many simply swayed in place and took turns holding up their sleeping partner. Dance marathons could be stressful, but people participated in them frequently because prizes at the larger dance contests could be up to several thousand dollars. These rewards were huge during the Great Depression and would allow marathon dancers to feed their families or pay

Dance marathons in the 1930s often went on for so long that participants fell asleep on the dance floor. Shown here are couples trying to keep moving after more than 900 hours, or about 37 days, of dancing.

PAST MEETS PRESENT: DANCE MARATHONS

Today, less risky versions of dance marathons exist as fundraising events; typically, these contents run between 4 and 24 hours, in contrast to the weeks-long extravaganzas of the 1930s. Because they're shorter and safer, they're generally more fun. During the Great Depression, entering a dance marathon and staying moving was sometimes seen as a necessary chore. The marathons provided food for the contestants and a warm place to stay in addition to the possibility of a cash prize, so for some people, entering one and staying on the dance floor as long as possible was the only way they could survive.

Today, in contrast, people generally enter a dance marathon to raise money for a cause they believe in, and they have fun competing against other dancers. One dance marathon is hosted in association with the Miracle Network, which raises money for Children's Miracle Network Hospitals. People can apply on the organization's website to host or attend a marathon in their town. In addition to dancing, these events often feature games, food, and guest speakers.

their rent. Even if they didn't win, a couple that entered a marathon would have access to food and shelter for as long as they could keep moving.

The problem with dance marathons was that the participants often risked their health—and occasionally, even their lives. Couples were allowed breaks to take a short nap, eat, or go to the bathroom, but only as long as one of them remained moving at all times on the dance floor. Taking care of basic necessities in shifts this way and remaining in motion at nearly all times eventually took a toll on participants; in one extreme case, a contestant named Homer Morehouse died from exhaustion after dancing for 87 hours. Because of these risks, many places eventually outlawed these contests.

Helping Women and People of Color

Although the Depression hit everyone hard, some people suffered much more than others. For example, men who were lucky enough to keep their jobs still struggled to make ends meet, but not as much as men who lost their jobs or families who became homeless did. Women, immigrants, and people of color suffered from economic hardship while also enduring prejudice and discrimination that American-born white men rarely saw. Even before the Depression hit, these groups had difficulty getting ahead in life. Each extra category increased the difficulty a person faced. For example, while white American-born women certainly faced discrimination, white immigrant women faced even more, and women of color—whether immigrant or native-born—faced the most. When the financial ruin of the Depression hit, these groups were affected even more severely than white men.

President Roosevelt and his New Deal tried to institute programs and initiatives that would aid these groups. Though there was some social progress toward equality—the most famous example was Frances Perkins, the first female cabinet member in US history—many of these plans failed to make much of an impact. With the weight of the Great Depression bearing down on every American, the dominant class of white, American-born men was generally able to maintain its major share of power.

Success for Some

Despite the significant obstacles, some members of these disadvantaged groups were able to make measurable gains during the 1930s. In the case of American women, these gains mainly took the form of ceremonial or formal appointments by the president to various governmental posts. Generally, these positions were high in rank and highly visible. In addition to Frances Perkins, there was Ruth Bryan Owen, the first female ambassador, and Florence E. Allen, the first woman to preside as chief judge of a federal circuit court of appeals. Women were also in charge of some of the New Deal programs. Hallie Flanagan directed the Federal Theatre Project, for instance, and Mary McLeod Bethune held a high position in the National Youth

THEY MADE HISTORY: MARY MCLEOD BETHUNE

In the United States, one of the leading black female figures of the 1920s and 1930s was Mary McLeod Bethune. She was born in South Carolina in 1875 to two former slaves who had been freed at the end of the American Civil War. A brilliant and hard-working student, young Mary attended Scotia Seminary, a college in North Carolina. She soon earned a reputation as a high-quality educator. In 1904, Bethune established a school in Daytona Beach, Florida, which eventually became Bethune-Cookman College. She served as president of the college from 1923 until 1942, then again from 1946 to 1947. Partly because of her friendship with First Lady Eleanor Roosevelt, FDR placed Bethune in charge of the Negro Affairs Division in a New Deal program, the NYA. This made Bethune the first black American to hold a head position in a government agency. In 1935, she founded the National Council of Negro Women, an organization dedicated to the advancement of black women in America, and in 1944, she helped found the United Negro College Fund (UNCF) to help pay for black students' college tuition. Bethune died in 1955. She is remembered today not only for her achievements as an educator but also for her work in breaking down racial and gender barriers in the federal government.

Administration (NYA). Bethune was also the first black American to serve in such a high position in a federal government agency.

The most visible woman in the government during the Depression era was the First Lady of the United States, Eleanor Roosevelt. As one historian explained, Eleanor did a great deal to advance the status of American women:

> *[Her] commitment to women's full … participation in American politics and business was intense, and she worked with women's*

groups around the nation to build their political base ... In her first year as First Lady, [she] worked hard to keep women involved in establishing and evaluating the New Deal ... [she] assembled a list of women qualified for executive level appointments, urged the Roosevelt administration to hire them, and, when their suggestions did not get a fair hearing, did not hesitate to take their ideas to FDR.[5]

Outside of these high positions, however, the progress for women in America wasn't as advanced. In fact, the vast majority of American women made only small gains against widespread prejudices during the 1930s. This was partly because of longstanding social traditions that viewed men as the main breadwinners and heads of households. During the Great Depression, American manufacturing industries sustained severe economic damage, and that put men out of work. However, because women worked in other industries—commonly as receptionists or secretaries—their jobs were more stable. Between 1930 and 1940, in fact, the total employment of women actually increased. For this reason, some people thought that working women were taking jobs away from men, thereby hurting both families and the country. This sexist attitude explains why a 1939 survey "showed that 84 percent of insurance companies, 65 percent of banks, and 63 percent of public utilities had restrictions on married women working."[6] Some men were particularly hostile toward female employment. "Simply fire the women, who shouldn't be working anyway, and hire the men," journalist Norman Cousins wrote. "Presto! No unemployment. No relief rolls. No Depression."[7]

Scorning "Women's Work"

Ignorant statements such as the one Cousins made were common at the time, as many men felt powerless and looked for someone to blame. In reality, women almost exclusively did work that men didn't traditionally do. Because "women's work" was scorned by most men and seen as something that would make them less manly, many men refused to take such jobs, even if they had to remain unemployed and stand in bread lines instead.

During the Depression, unemployed women married to employed men were lucky enough to receive at least some financial support, although two incomes were better than one. Single women, however, needed jobs to support themselves just as badly as unemployed men did. Shown here are unemployed single women protesting to draw attention to their need.

Furthermore, the few women who were employed to do jobs that men were willing to take made considerably less money for the same exact work. The average annual pay of an employed woman in the 1930s was $525, compared with $1,027 for a man. Even many of Roosevelt's New Deal programs, including those headed by women, discriminated against women by failing to grant them pay equal to that of men. While wage-earning codes set by the NRA did help women workers by guaranteeing them a minimum wage, the minimum wage for men was much higher than the one for women.

Even though women's employment increased during the Depression, working women were still the minority. Many stayed home to cook, clean, raise children, work in farm fields, and do the best they could to make ends meet in the cruel economy. Though these women had done nothing to threaten the male job market, they were nonetheless victimized by deeply ingrained gender biases. For example, the Social Security Act initially treated women unfairly. When it was first enacted, the program helped only the wage earners themselves, who were almost always men. If a male worker died, his stay-at-home wife couldn't collect any of his benefits and found herself shut out of the system. Even when the government amended the law in 1939, unemployed widows were only permitted to collect a certain percentage of their deceased husband's benefits.

Whether they worked or not, American women in the 1930s were still widely considered second-class citizens. They undoubtedly benefited to some degree from the New Deal, but in general, their lives were only improved minimally. Issues of gender equality took a place of lesser importance in the face of economic catastrophe.

A Powerful Prejudice

People of color—both men and women—also suffered discrimination throughout the Depression, just as they had before it. America was not even 80 years removed from the abolition of slavery, and old discriminatory practices were still in place. This was especially true in the South, but all over the country, black people were almost always considered inferior to whites.

At the height of the Depression, when jobs were few and far between, many racist white people resented seeing black people get any kind of work. These white people believed they should have the first pick of all jobs. Similarly to women, before the onset of the Depression, black citizens frequently did jobs that many white men would not take, including jobs as a domestic servant, elevator operator, garbage collector, waiter, street cleaner, and train porter. When the economy collapsed, more whites were willing to take these jobs, and many demanded that black workers quit or be fired to make way for them. Some white people in Atlanta, Georgia, began using the racially discriminatory slogan, "No Jobs for [Blacks] Until Every White Man Has a Job."[8] This kind of prejudice was widespread and was only made worse by the Depression.

One result of such blatant racism was that in the Depression era, black people were frequently the last to get hired and the first to get fired. Their employment opportunities were virtually nonexistent, and any job they managed to land was highly unstable. In 1932, with the country's overall unemployment figure nearing 25 percent, the unemployment rate for black people was already 50 percent. At the start of the 1930s, a large portion of America's 12 million black citizens lived in rural areas, and millions worked in agricultural jobs. Fewer than 15 percent of black farmers owned the land they worked on. The vast majority were sharecroppers, meaning they worked on someone else's land in exchange for a portion of the profits. Essentially, this system was a legal extension of slavery,

During the Great Depression, black people generally suffered more than white people because of racism and discrimination.

as most sharecroppers were kept constantly in debt to the people whose land they worked.

As in most American industries during the Depression, agricultural production fell on hard times, and many landowners evicted their tenants. Because such a large portion of the black population worked as sharecroppers, their sudden job loss was a huge blow to national unemployment averages. Moreover, even those who kept their agricultural jobs were paid less money than white people who did similar jobs. In 1934, black farmers had an average income of $200 or less per year; this was not nearly enough to live a good life, and far less money than white farmers earned.

Trying to Address Racism

Though racism, prejudice, and discrimination against black Americans were still strong during the Depression, there was some major progress toward racial equality during the 1930s. Harold Ickes, in particular, was a prominent advocate for racial equality in the United States. He wrote, "The Negro has met with many abuses and obstacles … For generations, he has been exploited by corrupt politicians, who have bought his vote or have made him promises which were never expected to be kept."[9] Under some of Roosevelt's New Deal programs in the middle of the decade, black citizens made more economic and social gains than they had in the entire seven decades following the Civil War. These gains were still not nearly enough to eliminate prejudice; when the Depression ended in the early 1940s, black people were still second-class citizens suffering under an enormous load of racial discrimination. However, Roosevelt's administration and the New Deal did make a difference. In fact, some historians trace the beginnings of the civil rights movement, which blossomed in the 1950s and 1960s, back to the mid-1930s.

Though many of his top advisers supported more equal rights for black citizens, it's still unclear what views Roosevelt held personally. In his public speeches and policies, he at least attempted to treat black Americans more fairly, more equally, and with more dignity than they'd been shown in the past. Roosevelt abolished

FROM THE SOURCE: PREJUDICE DURING THE GREAT DEPRESSION

One white man who lived through the Depression was shocked by the open racism of his fellow Americans when he traveled to the South to help the government build a camp for poor black people. He remembered some of the prejudicial remarks he overheard before the camp was constructed:

> *When the government came in and started to build a model camp for Negroes, with screened shelters and shower baths and flush toilets, and an infirmary, a community center, a school and playgrounds ... [local whites] raised hell. What was the government's idea anyway, ruining the rental value of their [homes]? ... Besides, the Negroes wouldn't use the camp, [the whites argued]. They liked to be dirty; they liked to be diseased; they liked to be vicious.*
>
> *When the [whites] saw the Government was going ahead anyway, they said: You'll have to hire a bunch of camp guards, white guards, and have them control the camp with clubs and pistols or the Negroes won't pay the rent. Or they'll stop working entirely and they'll take the camp to pieces.*[1]

The racially motivated fears of these white protestors were nothing but discriminatory myths. When the government did open the camp for homeless black Americans, its new, all-black governing council ran it efficiently and well, and the camp provided a clean, safe home for many black people who had become victims of the Great Depression.

1. Quoted in Studs Terkel, *Hard Times: An Oral History of the Great Depression* (New York, NY: New Press, 2005), p. 280.

segregation in federal offices in Washington, DC, and began to racially integrate the armed forces. He also appointed black men and women as advisers on race relations in the main offices of several New Deal programs.

The president made these moves, which were revolutionary in the 1930s, partly because he had surrounded himself with progressive, fair-minded individuals such as Ickes. They advised him politically, but Roosevelt's attitudes about race relations and equality were influenced even more by his wife. Most of Eleanor's knowledge about black problems came from her close friendships with Mary McLeod Bethune and Walter White. White was a leader of the National Association for the Advancement of Colored People (NAACP), which had been established in 1909. Some historical reports indicate that

Eleanor Roosevelt (*center*) championed equal rights for black people after her friend, Mary McLeod Bethune (*left*), educated her about the problems black citizens had faced for generations.

Eleanor was responsible for bringing the need for equality to FDR's attention. She is also credited with convincing Roosevelt to make his New Deal programs more inclusive of disadvantaged groups.

As a result, many of Roosevelt's job programs, such as the PWA and CCC, became small but important instruments of equality. These agencies mandated equal pay for equal work, even across racial boundaries. Many whites complained about this equal treatment, claiming that their labor was worth more than the labor of black men. Advocates for equality responded by pointing out that black workers had to support their families just as white workers did. Roosevelt responded to racist remarks and demands by employing hundreds of thousands of black men through the CCC and appointing a number of other people of color to high-ranking positions throughout his New Deal initiatives.

Though some of the changes the administration made were undoubtedly positive, they were still relatively small victories for black Americans. Racism was still alive and well in the United States, and no matter how much Roosevelt and his chief administrators tried to avoid it, blatant discrimination existed in the New Deal programs. Black people faced discrimination in many areas, including hiring, firing, wages, and housing, as well as in other areas. For example, black people benefited from loans obtained from the Farm Security Administration (FSA), a New Deal agency that lent money to needy farmers. Nearly a quarter of the FSA's loans went to black people. However, because they were already at an economic disadvantage compared to white people, historians argue that even this proportion was insufficient.

New Deal administrators typically responded to accusations of racism by saying that the fault lay with the old prejudices of individuals, not with Roosevelt's government. Even the most progressive minds in the federal government realized that centuries of prejudice couldn't be dismantled overnight, and they undoubtedly had biases they weren't even aware of. However, they did more during the 1930s than some administrations in past and future eras did.

Longstanding prejudices against Native Americans were also impossible to erase quickly. Government officials did, however, try to

Shown here is John Collier (*center*) with the chiefs of the Blackfoot group in 1934. As the US Commissioner of Indian Affairs, Collier met with Native Americans to discuss legislation that would affect them.

make it easier for Native Americans to integrate into mainstream society. By 1929, many of them had already been confined to reservations for several decades. During those years, the federal government had been pursuing a policy of assimilation: slowly trying to absorb Native Americans into white society. The policy was poorly applied, was not very successful, intensified prejudice against Native Americans, and had racist motivations—the government was pushing assimilation so it could eliminate traditional Native American cultures. Because of this discrimination, Native Americans were already at a disadvantage when the Great Depression hit.

Their situation began to improve slightly with the launch of the New Deal. John Collier, an open-minded and progressive social worker, became the US Commissioner of Indian Affairs. Collier recognized that the assimilation policy was racist and destructive, so

HISTORY HAPPENED HERE: OKLAHOMA

In 1930, a drought hit the area of the United States known as the Southern Plains, which was made up of parts of Oklahoma, Kansas, Nebraska, and northern Texas. The drought, high winds, and several unwise farming practices caused the soil to turn to dust, so this area became known as the Dust Bowl. Of course, the Dust Bowl and the stock market crash weren't related, but the timing was exceptionally bad. The Dust Bowl heightened the effects of the Great Depression for many farming families. While people who lived in cities had a variety of places close by where they could try to find work, farmers had to leave their homes—and often their entire state—to try to find a job.

Thanks to several New Deal initiatives as well as the natural end of the drought in 1939, the environmental disaster of the Dust Bowl was eventually reversed. Today, the states that were affected by the Dust Bowl have thriving farms and cities. For example, Oklahoma offers tourist attractions such as the Oklahoma City Zoo, the Museum of the Great Plains in Lawton, the Gilcrease Museum—featuring art and history from white settlers as well as Native American cultures—in Tulsa, the Cherokee Heritage Center in the Cherokee capital city of Tahlequah, and the Myriad Botanical Gardens in Oklahoma City.

he launched a new policy that aimed to preserve traditional Native American cultures. This goal was the central feature of the 1934 Indian Reorganization Act (IRA). It strengthened tribal governments, encouraged the expansion of Native American commercial endeavors to create self-reliance, and helped secure education loans to help young Native Americans afford college.

Despite its positive goals, the IRA was aimed mostly at the long term. This was an issue because in the middle of the Depression, what many Native Americans needed most was jobs. To address this short-term issue, Collier organized the Indian Emergency

In the Dust Bowl, high winds created dust drifts such as this one, sometimes blocking doors and windows. The dust also got into houses and covered furniture, floors, people, and food with a layer of sand.

Conservation Work (IECW) program, funded as a branch of the CCC. Thousands of Native Americans were employed on or near reservations to plant forests, combat soil erosion, and build roads and fire lookout stations. Though it was enacted on a much smaller scale than the general CCC, the IECW was highly successful among unemployed and impoverished Native Americans in the 1930s.

Immigrants and Okies

Not all prejudice during the Great Depression was racial. In fact, some white people were discriminated against nearly as much as people of color during the 1930s, although they had a slight advantage in the fact that they hadn't been suffering such discrimination for nearly as long. In the three decades before the onset of the Depression, millions of immigrants had come to the United States from countries such as Italy, Ireland, Greece, Poland, Hungary, Germany, and Russia. Although they were mainly white, they received a mixed reception from American citizens even before the Depression hit. Some people welcomed them, helping them assimilate and respecting their various international cultures. Others, however, saw them as intruders who were trying to steal jobs from "real Americans." This attitude only intensified during the Depression, as competition for jobs increased among all people living in the United States. Some immigrants, and even their American-born children, were the targets of fierce racial discrimination all across the United States. This damaging treatment could range anywhere from name-calling to murder.

Even some whites who were not immigrants were discriminated against during the Depression, based partially on the fear that they were trying to take other people's jobs. The "Okies" were the most famous example. This name came from the fact that many of them were from Oklahoma. Okies were the main victims of the Dust Bowl, since the dust storms hit Oklahoma especially hard. The worst of these storms, which came to be known as Black Sunday because the dust clouds blotted out the sun, occurred on April 14, 1935. More than 500,000 citizens of the region fled to other states to look for work. An estimated 15 percent of Oklahoma residents, along with people from other states affected by the Dust Bowl, moved to California, and Okie soon became a derogatory term. "They were promptly stereotyped, exactly like a racial minority," wrote Carey McWilliams, who was the child of migrant workers in the 1930s. "They were [supposedly] shiftless and lazy and irresponsible and had too many children ... Once I went into the foyer of this third-rate [movie theater] in [California] and I saw a sign: Negroes and Okies upstairs."[10]

The problems migrant workers faced were brought to the public's attention by John Steinbeck's 1939 novel, *The Grapes of Wrath*, and by the movie version made shortly afterwards. Both showed how poor migrant workers experienced intense poverty and prejudice during the Depression years.

How You See History

1. Imagine you and your family can't buy anything at all for the next two weeks. How would you make what you already have last?
2. How did racism and sexism make the Depression worse for certain groups?
3. Why were Okies more heavily discriminated against than other American-born white people who were also suffering during the Depression?

1941

CHAPTER FIVE

A LASTING LEGACY

The New Deal didn't put an end to the Depression—especially not by the time Roosevelt's first term as president ended in 1936. However, many people felt hopeful with concrete plans in place and wanted the New Deal to continue. Roosevelt's critics argued that the government was getting too involved in people's lives, but his supporters responded that unemployment had decreased by almost 10 percent since he took office. Because of this, they argued that it had been necessary for the government to get involved to save the economy and get it back on track.

The numbers were convincing. Roosevelt won his second term almost unopposed, and his victory remains one of the largest margins of victory in US history. During his next four years, his administration worked to refine and broaden existing New Deal programs while also introducing new and diverse initiatives. He was so successful that he was elected for a third term in 1940—the only person to have ever achieved this. Entering this third term, Roosevelt and his advisers were still looking for ways to end the economic crisis. Though the New Deal's programs had been functioning as promised for six years, unemployment was decreasing but still high, and the economy was growing, but not quickly. A new world war would change that.

Into War and Out of the Depression

One of the reasons for the steadily declining unemployment rate was an increase in manufacturing production. In 1939, most of Europe had been

◀ Roosevelt was the only president to ever win a third and fourth term in office. Shown here is his third inauguration.

plunged into World War II. Though the United States was not yet directly involved, it began supplying Great Britain and its allies with large amounts of industrial and military equipment. As the war went on, production requirements increased, creating many new jobs for Americans in the process. By 1941, the level of industrial production in the United States was even higher than it had been early in 1929, before the stock market crashed and set off the Great Depression. American industrial output continued to grow exponentially after the Japanese attack on Pearl Harbor in December 1941, which pulled the United States fully into the ongoing world war. Building up the nation's armed forces was an extremely powerful catalyst for economic recovery.

Under these circumstances, the question for economists and historians became: How much did the New Deal itself contribute to the national return to prosperity? Some experts have concluded that Roosevelt's policies and programs to fight the Depression were failures. They argue that he conducted a large, expensive, and ultimately ineffective experiment. In their view, he and his New Dealers continually failed to balance the federal budget, greatly increased the national debt, and expanded the federal government into an inappropriately huge bureaucracy. Other historians have been more positive in their analysis of the New Deal. They argue that its various programs helped increase the national average income and employed millions of jobless, desperate people. They also point out that the economy started to grow again in 1938—a year before World War II was officially declared. Some speculate that the New Deal policies would have helped it continue to grow, while others believe it would have continued to struggle if the United States hadn't gotten involved in the war. Most importantly, though, Roosevelt and the New Deal restored the country's morale, which had reached an all-time low during the Depression's early years.

Moreover, Roosevelt's defenders have pointed out that there is no way to tell what the New Deal might have accomplished if the war had not erupted. In fact, experts have argued that a few more years of vigorous New Deal programs could potentially have brought the economy back on track. It's true that the government borrowed a lot of money to fund its New Deal projects, which created an enormous budget deficit. Similarly, however, the government borrowed a great deal of money to fund its costly war effort, which also created a deficit.

FROM THE SOURCE: AN INFAMOUS DAY

When World War II first began, many people in the United States supported staying out of the actual fight, although they were willing to provide their allies with supplies. However, once Pearl Harbor was attacked, that attitude changed. On December 8, 1941, FDR gave one of his most historic speeches. In part, he said:

> *Yesterday, December 7th, 1941—a date which will live in infamy—the United States of America was suddenly and deliberately attacked by naval and air forces of the Empire of Japan ... The facts of yesterday and today speak for themselves. The people of the United States have already formed their opinions and well understand the implications to the very life and safety of our nation ... No matter how long it may take us to overcome this premeditated invasion, the American people in their righteous might will win through to absolute victory. I believe that I interpret the will of the Congress and of the people when I assert that we will not only defend ourselves to the uttermost, but will make it very certain that this form of treachery shall never again endanger us ... I ask that Congress declare that since the unprovoked and dastardly attack by Japan on Sunday, December 7th, 1941, a state of war has existed between the United States and the Japanese Empire.*[1]

1. Quoted in Jennifer Rosenberg, "FDR's 'Day of Infamy' Speech," ThoughtCo., modified March 14, 2019, www.thoughtco.com/day-of-infamy-speech-1779637.

Helping Citizens

Regardless of the immediate results of the New Deal, there is no doubt that the Depression and Roosevelt's programs impacted the United States in significant and enduring ways. His reforms were revolutionary at the time, his programs were bold, and his strategies were unique. He served as president for more years than anyone else, and after the

In contrast to the 1930s, the years after World War II were a time of great prosperity. While this was mainly due to the production boom of the war, some historians believe the New Deal helped.

1947 introduction of the 22nd Amendment, which limits the president to two terms in office, no one else will ever match his total.

In the long run, various large-scale social programs, including Social Security and the FDIC, remained in place, and they've become accepted fixtures of American life. Not long after the United States escaped from the Great Depression, politicians from both major parties, Democrats and Republicans, accepted many of the bold and formerly controversial components of the New Deal, including laws for minimum wages, limits on the number of hours employees could work in a week, and the insurance of bank deposits. In the 21st century, some of these topics have come up for debate among politicians again, but many programs are still widely supported by the American public.

Before the beginning of the Depression and the creation of the New Deal to fight it, the United States had no national old-age pension plan, no aid for dependent children, no federal housing, no federal compensation for the unemployed, no federal school lunch program for children from low-income families, no minimum wage requirements, and no government welfare system. The New Deal laid the groundwork and provided the basic ideals and structure for that aid.

One of the major changes in the New Deal was the elimination of child labor. It also prohibited sweatshops that exploited men, women, and children by paying them barely enough to stay alive and forcing them to work in substandard conditions. These new laws were beneficial to low-income Americans, both immediately and in the long term.

PAST MEETS PRESENT: DEPRESSION MENTALITY

The Great Depression took a lifelong psychological toll on many people. Even after it ended and jobs and money became abundant again, many people continued to save. Some people were too scared to use banks ever again, even after the FDIC was created. Some refused to buy things they needed or wanted even if they had enough money to do so. Some saved scraps of paper, bits of string, and other odds and ends out of fear that they would someday not have enough money to buy such things when they needed them. Most members of younger generations didn't understand this mentality; they were sometimes confused or frustrated when their parents or grandparents insisted on saving everything unnecessarily.

However, since the Great Recession, younger generations have started adopting a similar mentality, or thought process. According to a 2014 report by the Union Bank of Switzerland (UBS), millennials—people born between 1981 and 1996—are "the most fiscally [financially] conservative generation since the Great Depression."[1] Millennials, who have had trouble finding jobs since the recession started, are more likely to save their money than to invest it or spend it, in contrast to older people. According to researcher Emily Pachuta,

> *Conventional wisdom has categorized Millennials as "entitled" and "lazy," because they have more than their parents and grandparents did, but this study counters that hypothesis ... They're conservative, similar to the WWII generation coming out of the Great Depression ... working hard for their wealth and success, making sacrifices, because they believe their goals are achievable.*[2]

1. Quoted in Hal M. Bundrick, "Gen Y Develops a Depression-Era Mentality," The Street, January 28, 2014, www.thestreet.com/story/12784855/1/gen-y-develops-depression-era-mentality.html.

2. Quoted in Bundrick, "Gen Y Develops a Depression-Era Mentality."

Most of the New Deal programs that still exist in some form as of 2020 are part of the national economy. The 1933 Securities Act, for example, made people who run companies criminally liable for misinformation in their financial statements. The 1934 Securities Exchange Act established a federal commission to oversee the stock market with the goal of preventing another massive stock market crash. Also in 1934, the Federal Housing Administration (FHA) made one aspect of the American dream more accessible: owning a home. The FHA is a government organization that helps potential homeowners get access to mortgages or other loans that are more affordable than what banks offer. Widespread homeownership is an important component of a thriving national economy, and the FHA has been successful for more than 80 years.

Back on Track

The most obvious effects of the Great Depression were visible and material. Millions of people lost their jobs, went hungry, and became homeless. The numbers alone, however, cannot tell the entire story of how difficult the 1930s were in America. Alongside the national economic depression rose a sort of national psychological depression: People lost hope in themselves, their leaders, and their country. For years, especially from 1929 to 1932, it seemed like there was no end in sight for millions of struggling Americans. When President Franklin D. Roosevelt took office, things began to change.

The historical significance of the New Deal is impossible to ignore. The main benefit of these programs was that they introduced hope and stability back into the general American populace. Millions of people were put back to work, and they could suddenly provide for their families again. Roosevelt's administration reminded the nation that they could rise to any challenge—and overcome it—just as their ancestors did.

How You See History

1. How much do you think the New Deal helped the economy?
2. Do you think the United States could have recovered from the Great Depression without World War II?
3. What's your opinion of the New Deal policies that are still in place?

TIMELINE

March 4, 1929
Herbert Hoover takes office.

October 24, 1929
The American stock market crashes, plunging the country into the Great Depression.

June 1930
Hoover signs the Smoot-Hawley Tariff Act; the Dust Bowl drought begins.

June 6, 1932
Hoover signs the Revenue Act to increase taxes.

1933
Franklin Delano Roosevelt (FDR) begins his first term as president and launches the New Deal; unemployment reaches its peak at 24.9 percent.

April 14, 1934
Black Sunday—the worst storm of the Dust Bowl—occurs.

April 27, 1935
FDR passes the Soil Conservation Act to help farmers use more sustainable methods.

1935
The Supreme Court declares the National Recovery Administration unconstitutional; the Works Progress Administration is created; the Social Security Act is passed.

1937
FDR takes office for his second term and continues passing New Deal legislation.

1938

The economy begins to grow again.

1939

World War II officially begins in Europe; the United States starts supplying its allies with weapons; the Dust Bowl drought ends.

1941

FDR begins his unprecedented third term; Japan attacks Pearl Harbor, causing the United States to declare war.

1954

The stock market officially recovers.

NOTES

Introduction: A Worldwide Struggle

1. "The Great Depression," United States Holocaust Memorial Museum, accessed December 16, 2019, encyclopedia.ushmm.org/content/en/article/the-great-depression.
2. Quoted in Studs Terkel, *Hard Times: An Oral History of the Great Depression* (New York, NY: New Press, 2005), p. 45.
3. Quoted in William Dudley, ed., *The Great Depression: Opposing Viewpoints* (San Diego, CA: Greenhaven Press, 1994), p. 36.
4. Robert S. McElvaine, *The Great Depression: America, 1929–1941* (New York, NY: Three Rivers Press, 2009), p. xi.

Chapter One: Crash and Burn

1. Howard Zinn, *A People's History of the United States* (New York, NY: HarperCollins, 2005), p. 373.
2. Samuel E. Morison, *The Oxford History of the American People* (New York, NY: Oxford University Press, 1965), p. 937.
3. Quoted in Studs Terkel, *Hard Times: An Oral History of the Great Depression* (New York, NY: New Press, 2005), p. 66.
4. Gerald W. Johnson, *Franklin D. Roosevelt: Portrait of a Great Man* (New York, NY: William Morrow, 1967), pp. 119–20.
5. Quoted in Terkel, *Hard Times*, p. 425.

Chapter Two: Presidential Failures and Successes

1. Quoted in Samuel E. Morison, *The Oxford History of the American People* (New York, NY: Oxford University Press, 1965), p. 945.
2. Quoted in "Document: 'Principles and Ideals of the United States Government,'" Teaching American History, accessed December 16, 2019, teachingamericanhistory.org/library/document/principles-and-ideals-of-the-united-states-government.
3. Herbert Hoover, "February 3, 1931: Statement on Unemployment Relief," Miller Center, accessed December 16, 2019, millercenter.org/the-presidency/presidential-speeches/february-3-1931-statement-unemployment-relief.

4. Quoted in "Document: Acceptance Speech at the Democratic Convention (1932)," Teaching American History, accessed December 16, 2019, teachingamericanhistory.org/library/document/acceptance-speech-at-the-democratic-convention-1932.
5. Quoted in Robert Lynn Fuller, *"Phantom of Fear": The Banking Panic of 1933* (Jefferson, NC: McFarland, 2012), p. 186.
6. Franklin Delano Roosevelt, "First Fireside Chat: Delivered 12 March 1933, Washington D.C.," American Rhetoric, modified February 26, 2017, www.americanrhetoric.com/speeches/fdrfirstfiresidechat.html.
7. Robert S. McElvaine, *The Great Depression: America, 1929–1941* (New York, NY: Three Rivers Press, 2009), p. 149.

Chapter Three: Helping a Nation Recover

1. Quoted in Studs Terkel, *Hard Times: An Oral History of the Great Depression* (New York, NY: New Press, 2005), pp. 247–48.
2. Quoted in Arthur M. Schlesinger Jr., *The Age of Roosevelt, Volume II: The Coming of the New Deal, 1933–1935* (Boston, MA: Mariner Books, 2003), p. 311.
3. Quoted in Terkel, *Hard Times*, p. 249.

Chapter Four: Living Through the Depression

1. Lorena A. Hickok, "To Eleanor Roosevelt," in Richard Lowitt and Maurine Beasley, eds., *One Third of a Nation: Lorena Hickok Reports on the Great Depression* (Chicago, IL: University of Illinois Press, 1983), p. 60.
2. Robert S. McElvaine, *The Great Depression: America, 1929–1941* (New York, NY: Three Rivers Press, 2009), p. 172.
3. Joseph L. Heffernan, "The Hungry City: A Mayor's Experience with Unemployment," in US Senate Committee on Labor and Public Welfare, *Selected Readings in Employment and Manpower, Volumes 1–5* (Washington, DC: US Government Printing Office, 1964), p. 1722.
4. Quoted in McElvaine, *The Great Depression*, p. 173–74.
5. "Eleanor Roosevelt and the Women's Movement," Eleanor Roosevelt Papers Project, accessed December 17, 2019, www2.gwu.edu/~erpapers/teachinger/lesson-plans/notes-er-and-womens-movement.cfm.

6. Quoted in Mary Eleanor Triece, *On the Picket Line: Strategies of Working-Class Women During the Depression* (Chicago, IL: University of Illinois Press, 2007), p. 79.
7. Quoted in McElvaine, *The Great Depression*, p. 182.
8. Quoted in McElvaine, *The Great Depression*, p. 187.
9. Harold L. Ickes, "The Negro as a Citizen," in Howard Zinn, ed., *New Deal Thought* (Indianapolis, IN: Bobbs-Merrill, 1966), p. 341.
10. Quoted in Studs Terkel, *Hard Times: An Oral History of the Great Depression* (New York, NY: New Press, 2005), p. 243.

FOR MORE INFORMATION

Books: Nonfiction

Baxter, Roberta. *The Great Depression: A History Perspectives Book.* Ann Arbor, MI: Cherry Lake Publishing, 2015.

Cohen, Robert, ed., *Dear Mrs. Roosevelt: Letters from Children of the Great Depression.* Chapel Hill, NC: University of North Carolina Press, 2008.

Lüsted, Marcia Amidon, and Tom Casteel. *The Great Depression: Experience the 1930s from the Dust Bowl to the New Deal.* White River Junction, VT: Nomad Press, 2016.

Offord, Alexander. *The Causes of World War II.* St. Catharines, ON, Canada: Crabtree Publishing Company, 2016.

Otfinoski, Steven. *The Great Depression.* New York, NY: Scholastic, 2018.

Books: Fiction

Hesse, Karen. *Out of the Dust.* New York, NY: Scholastic, 1997.

Websites

BrainPOP

www.brainpop.com

A search for "Great Depression" on this website offers videos, quizzes, primary sources, and games on a variety of related topics, including the New Deal, Franklin and Eleanor Roosevelt, and life during the Depression.

BuzzFeed News: "These Pictures Capture the American Struggle During the Great Depression"

www.buzzfeednews.com/article/gabrielsanchez/american-dream-great-depression-photos

This collection of historical photographs from the book *A Vision Shared: A Classic Portrait of America 1935–1943* and their accompanying descriptions give a clear image of life during the Great Depression.

History.com: The Great Depression

www.history.com/topics/great-depression

Maintained by the History Channel, this website gives an informative overview of the Depression.

PBS: Riding the Rails Timeline

www.pbs.org/wgbh/americanexperience/features/timeline/rails-timeline

This timeline gives a detailed account of the important events of the 1930s.

INDEX

G

H

I

J

K

M

N

O

PHOTO CREDITS

Cover Transcendental Graphics/Getty Images; p. 4 Mario Tama/Getty Images; p. 7 IgorGolovniov/Shutterstock.com; pp. 10, 26, 34, 60, 68, 74 Everett Historical/Shutterstock.com; pp. 12, 42, 51, 79, 81 Bettmann/Bettmann/Getty Images; p. 15 Felix Lipov/Shutterstock.com; p. 18 Kirn Vintage Stock/Corbis via Getty Images; p. 22 dikobraziy/Shutterstock.com; pp. 24, 36 Courtesy of the Library of Congress; p. 32 Underwood Archives/Getty Images; p. 40 Stock Montage/Getty Images; p. 43 Craig F. Walker/The Denver Post via Getty Images; p. 46 Everett Collection Inc/Alamy Stock Photo; p. 49 Archive PL/Alamy Stock Photo; p. 52 Russ Heinl/Shutterstock.com; p. 57 Patrick Fallon/Bloomberg via Getty Images; pp. 63, 66 © Minnesota Historical Society/CORBIS/Corbis via Getty Images; p. 69 NY Daily News Archive via Getty Images; p. 76 MPI/Getty Images; p. 83 © CORBIS/Corbis via Getty Images; p. 86 Fox Photos/Getty Images; p. 90 Nina Leen/The LIFE Picture Collection via Getty Images.

ABOUT THE AUTHOR

Simon Pierce grew up in Jamestown, New York. He later moved to New York City and completed his education at NYU. He now lives in Brooklyn with his partner and their son. He has written for various health and wellness publications over the past seven years, and although this is his first history book, he has always considered himself to be a history buff. He and his family enjoy people-watching in the park or reading the names on cemetery headstones and inventing stories about them.